Learning to Lead

My Life and Meijer

Earl Holton

WITH GORDON OLSON

WILLIAM B. EERDMANS PUBLISHING COMPANY
GRAND RAPIDS, MICHIGAN

© 1999 Wm. B. Eerdmans Publishing Co.
255 Jefferson Ave. S.E., Grand Rapids, Michigan 49503 /
P.O. Box 163, Cambridge CB3 9PU U.K.

Printed in the United States of America

04 03 02 01 00 99   7 6 5 4 3 2 1

Library of Congress Cataloging-in-Publication Data

Photo Credits: p. 107 — Courtesy Public Museum of Grand
Rapids; p. 107 — Steve Richardson (courtesy Frederik
Meijer Gardens); p. 115 — John M. Brouwer (courtesy
Grand Rapids Press)

This book is dedicated to my family —

Donnalee,
Mike and Jo Anne,
Elizabeth and John,
Brian and Jackie,
Kimberly and Brian,
and my
grandchildren,

— and to all 79,000
Meijer team members,
who do such a good job serving our guests,
24 hours a day, 364 days a year.

CONTENTS

FOREWORD

Hank Meijer

Earl Holton is a reluctant witness to his own achievements. Because these achievements have distinguished him as one of the most influential figures in American mass retailing, those of us who know him are under a special obligation to share what we know.

For more than a dozen years, Earl and I have worked from offices a few paces apart. But for what seems like my lifetime — Earl joined Meijer the year I was born — he has loomed large in our world, a man worthy of every confidence and deference. For most of three decades, in the 1960s, 1970s, and 1980s, Earl, my father, Fred, and Harvey Lemmen were intimately involved in all of the company's strategic decisions. Their titles were interchangeable. No less weight was given to vice president of operations than to executive vice president or president. Earl served in each role in turn while a small supermarket chain ventured forth with a handful of pioneering "supercenters" and then continued to reinvent and redefine itself with each passing year.

Today, Meijer has emerged as one of the top 20 retailers in the United States and one of the top 50 in the world, while remaining, as few other companies on such lists have succeeded in remaining, privately owned — an extended family business. When Harvey Lemmen retired and Fred Meijer scaled back his day-to-day involvement, the culture of this company came more and more to bear the stamp of Earl Holton. Such is the nature of that culture, however, that to single out individuals from such an able team goes against the grain. The "we" that comes through time and again when Earl describes the actions of this company is the furthest thing from "we" as owners and senior officers. It is the "we" of a team. The company's achievements belong to all of our team members. Earl knows that in his bones. It is why he is so reluctant to place himself in the spotlight. And why it might be more accurate to think of him as first among equals.

Earl Holton was born in Manton, Michigan, in 1934, the same year Hendrik Meijer opened a small grocery store 90 miles south in Greenville. As Earl recounts in these pages, he began his career at Meijer in the chain's second, and smallest, store. (There were a total of six in 1952.) This was in Cedar Springs, Michigan, half an hour north of Grand Rapids before the US 131 expressway was built. He was eighteen, just out of high school, and newly married to the vivacious young woman who had worked across the street at the Cedar Café when he first met her. Cedar Springs was one of a string of small Michigan towns Earl had called home when growing up. His father, a Free Methodist minister, was shunted from church to church, town to town, with what seemed, to a growing boy, maddening frequency.

Earl talks about his first days as a grocery clerk, when he made a few mistakes and tried to quit before he thought he might be fired. He says the store manager kept him on because the country was fighting the Korean War and the store was short of help. Were that true — I don't think any of us believe it — it would still be the case that Earl was trying to set a higher standard for himself than anybody else would think to.

The dairy aisle ran with milk from bottles he'd broken because he tried to stack the crates higher and stock them faster. He was eager. He had found a place, so unlike the factory in Muskegon where he put in some frustrating weeks, where eagerness was a virtue, and your job was a task you did the best you knew how, not according to some standard of mediocrity established to keep lazier workers from looking bad.

It required no great vision to see that the young clerk

had promise. Certainly Hendrik Meijer and his son Fred saw this. Earl knew they saw it, and from that mutual awareness arose a mutual trust that stayed with him through different jobs and different stores, and through supervisors not always as appreciative of his talents as Hendrik and Fred proved to be.

He managed his first store in 1955, at the age of twenty-one. He was only twenty-six when he became district manager, responsible for a considerable portion of the chain's operations. One year later, in 1962, he oversaw the opening of the first three Thrifty Acres stores, the first of the modern Meijer supercenters.

Earl has never waited for challenges to come his way. He has anticipated them, prepared for them, surrounded himself with people who could surmount them — or who would give their all trying, without having to fear recrimination. It has been the company's good fortune, and Earl's, too, that the big idea Hendrik and Fred started with, along with the supercenter concept, was to trust other people to do their jobs and welcome those who could do them better than they could do them themselves. That made this company a ready arena for Earl. Soon the standards he met were the ones he set.

In 1980, Earl became president of Meijer. As his responsibilities expanded, he became — in an evolution that appears almost seamless — a teacher. He showed the company the importance of superior logistics and technology, and how to not just survive but flourish, despite a unionized environment, through sensitive labor relations. When negotiations got heated and tempers frayed, it was Earl who reminded the bargainers that their real task was not to win a battle of egos across a table, but to think of the best interests of Meijer team members. From his early days in operations, when the boy whose parents were teetotalers took charge of the company's liquor licenses, he came to understand the importance of government relations. As the company grew and public policy decisions affected it more and more, those early lessons informed his judgment.

Always sensitive to nuance, he comprehends better than most of us the ways of the politician and the bureaucrat.

He has always studied others. What makes each of us tick? What are our strengths and weaknesses?

He has a reputation, as so many executives do, of hating surprises. He wants to know what's next, and where we go from here. He has patience when some of us might be more impulsive. But he loves change. He wants to see things happen.

He will tell you that he is not a merchant. This might be a startling admission from the leader of a company that exists to sell people what they need and want. He is a merchant, surely, if only because he listens to the guest. But that noble title does not do justice to all he does. He succeeds in retailing because he creates an environment in which a team of merchants can and does flourish.

This is far more than just the story of an ambitious-clerk-makes-good. That vivacious girl behind the counter at the Cedar Cafe became Earl's wife and mother to their four children, some of whom have made and are making their own contributions to the Meijer team. Donnalee also became a respected leader in the volunteer community, a school board member, and a university trustee. Earl and Donnalee's children are grown, and the parents are now grandparents. So have things changed in nearly half a century. In between is his career. And how unusual it is for man and career to be so much in harmony. He stayed in one place for 46 years — and helped to dramatically change that place, to make it both a great place to work and a revolutionary force in American retailing

Once, when I was a boy and had just started working in the store, my father was away and Earl picked me up to bring me to work. I was eleven, maybe, and unaccustomed to wearing a tie. I think I grumbled a bit. But that was the dress code; I had to conform. It was a standard, and just because I was the boss's son, Earl was not about to let things slide.

By paying attention to detail while maintaining a detachment of daunting objectivity, Earl senses problems and opportunities and never loses sight of his larger goals. Just as he has set so many other goals for himself, he began early to ponder his transition from president and chief operating officer to vice chairman of Meijer. It was his goal — his decision. He is valued too much by Fred and the rest of us for it to be otherwise.

But now we all learn by seeing how he does this, too. Not least Jim McLean, of course, who succeeds Earl as president, but Fred, my brothers Doug and Mark, and I all appreciate the sensitive and dispassionate way this man of great intensity — the executive's euphemism for passion — has made way for his successor.

He calculates — in the very best sense of the word — and then acts. He shows us the way. He will tell you he learned it from others. Perhaps. I know we learn it from him.

Time after time, when a difficult question arises, the common refrain coming from Fred has been, "Check with Earl." Many things change — titles, dress codes, offices, certainly stores. But not the Eleventh Commandment of this earnest culture that its president bequeaths us: "Check with Earl."

If Earl could explain why this is so, he wouldn't. Certainly his father, the minister, was a powerful influence in his life. And in this book Earl talks of others: coaches, colleagues, family, and friends. Whatever the influences, he brings wisdom to bear in large ways and small. His judgment is a source of inestimable strength. The accumulated effect of wisdom joined to decisiveness, judgment to action, is leadership. Earl learned that. He has an instinct for it. The rest of us will bear witness while he tells his story.

PROLOGUE

Fred Meijer

I was pleased to be asked to write this prologue to a book about Earl Holton. Earl and I have worked through so many experiences that it is hard to know where to start and when to stop.

Earl and I come from very different backgrounds. However, we've never had a problem reaching a consensus on a multitude of issues.

Some of my most enjoyable times were Saturday mornings at the office, when we would just talk, often not concerning our jobs. These conversations gave us a greater understanding of each other.

From my point of view, working with Earl has been an extraordinary exercise in decision making. We've never had a problem saying, "We may not agree, but let's go your way. It won't kill the company." Often when we reached a decision, that understanding went unsaid.

My father was a tremendous business mentor and teacher. I have always tried to follow his example of how to deal with people and reach objectives. I hope I've been a good mentor to Earl. However, as with families, you start out being their teacher and mentor; then, in later years, they become your mentor and teacher. The same is surely true with Earl. He has been one of my best mentors — advisers — for many years now, as Harvey Lemmen was before him.

I've been very lucky to have fine family and business associates, people of intelligence, quality, and dedication. But Earl particularly has played a significant role. So it is a real pleasure to write about one of the finest, most capable executives I've known. If we as a team have done things worth doing, it is usually because Earl Holton has steered us in the right direction.

Thanks, Earl. It's been great fun and a great pleasure.

Acknowledgments

Earl Holton
Gordon Olson

Learning to Lead grew out of Earl Holton's desire to share lessons learned during his 46-year retailing career. Like Hendrik Meijer and Fred Meijer before him, he firmly believes in the importance of passing Meijer's corporate culture from generation to generation through stories and conversations. Thus, when Hank Meijer proposed a book based on his experiences, he readily agreed.

Many people assisted with *Learning to Lead*, making it a typical Meijer team effort. The book's foundation is a series of taped interviews with Earl, supplemented by conversations with several of Earl's family, friends, and fellow team members. Donnalee Holton, Fred Meijer, Harvey Lemmen, former Meijer president, Jim McLean, current president, Dave Perron, senior vice president for merchandising, Tom Riddle, vice president for human resource communications and services, and retired team member John VanKuiken willingly provided additional information and anecdotes. Gordon Olson conducted the interviews, assisted by Hank Meijer and Bill Smith, group vice president for Meijer's marketing and advertising department. Executive assistant Pam Kleibusch set up numerous meetings and interviews and coordinated the transcribing of several interview tapes.

When it came time for book design and production, Kurt Staal took over project direction. Todd Lewis and Jamie Barendsen handled the book's overall design and layout. Jim Connelly Studio produced the cover design. Robert Viol, who oversees Meijer's corporate archives, helped find several key documents and illustrative photographs.

Michelle O'Brien patiently transcribed several of the taped interviews, and Sharon Pawloski of the Cedar Springs Historical Society provided photographs from Earl's high school years. Ellen Arlinsky and Jeff Mulder edited each chapter to fix grammatical inconsistencies and create a smooth narrative.

To all these team members, we extend our appreciation for assistance and encouragement. For any errors or omissions that may persist despite their best efforts, we accept full responsibility.

Introduction

Earl Holton is a career Meijer man. He joined the company soon after graduating from high school and stayed until retirement. Starting as a general clerk in 1952, he moved up the corporate ladder to store manager, district manager, vice president, and finally, in 1980, company president. His is a classic success story of starting at the bottom and rising to the top.

"I've had one of the more unusual careers in the retail industry," he says. "I have worked for three generations of the same family." In these days of executive mobility, such a strong and long-lasting bond between employer and employee is remarkable.

In some privately held companies, the owners pressure non-family officers to move on if they draw the spotlight. But Earl's relationship with the Meijer family completely avoids these kinds of tensions. Throughout his 46 years at Meijer, Earl has wholly embraced the key components the company was founded on — unwavering commitment to guest service, quality merchandise, the well-being of all Meijer team members, and community organizations.

So close that outsiders often assumed he was a member of the Meijer family, Earl learned many of his management values over coffee sessions with Hendrik Meijer, who taught lesson after lesson through stories of how he grew the business from a single grocery store in Greenville into a regional chain of supermarkets. Later, Earl worked closely with Fred Meijer and other top executives as the company developed its Thrifty Acres model and expanded beyond West Michigan.

LEARNING TO LEAD • MY LIFE AND MEIJER

When Earl took over as president in 1980, he led the company through a phenomenal growth phase. During his tenure, Meijer opened dozens of stores in Ohio, Indiana, Kentucky, and Illinois, becoming one of the nation's largest retailers. At the same time, Earl also laid the groundwork for further growth. A redefined store design, solid infrastructure, and skilled team have prepared Meijer well for retailing in the twenty-first century.

Learning to Lead is not an autobiography, since Earl did not want to focus all the attention on himself. Nor is it a narrative history of Meijer. Rather, it is a collection of stories that highlights lessons learned along a life's journey. Stories are one of the most effective and entertaining methods of explaining a corporate culture. In *Learning to Lead*, Earl uses the power of stories to reveal the principles that have successfully shaped and guided Meijer.

A careful listener and keen observer, Earl learned his management and personnel skills on the job instead of in the classroom. While other corporate presidents studied for bachelor's and master's degrees, Earl sought the advice of his mentors — his father, teachers, Hendrik and Fred Meijer among them. When he did make mistakes, he took care never to repeat them. Earl graduated with honors from the school of hard knocks, and Meijer willingly paid the tuition.

Earl also sought guidance from the best minds in a number of fields. A reader with wide-ranging tastes, he supplemented the lessons learned each day at work with the knowledge found in biographies, social commentaries, and business literature.

For five months, I met regularly with Earl, Hank Meijer, and Bill Smith. In the tradition of Hendrik Meijer, Earl taught us about the Meijer way of doing business by sharing stories of his experiences over the last 46 years. Those discussions resulted in the book you're reading now.

Readers inside and outside Meijer will enjoy this insider's perspective of one of West Michigan's greatest companies. Meijer team members will chuckle when Earl describes how his overzealous attitude led, early in his career, to a broken door, lots of spilled milk, and an attempt to quit before he could be fired. Stories highlighting the importance of rapid and efficient distribution will win nods from the same group.

Meijer guests will enjoy stories of how, on many occasions, Earl challenged the status quo. And I think they'll be surprised to learn that the company nearly went bankrupt inventing the Thrifty Acres concept, then experienced financial strains again five years later expanding that concept outside the West Michigan market.

My sessions with Earl clearly demonstrated the value of oral traditions in a corporate setting. Storytelling is encouraged at Meijer. Hank Meijer, Hendrik's grandson, penned a biography of his namesake titled *Thrifty Years*. Fred Meijer's recollections and speeches are available in *Fred Meijer: In His Own Words* and a companion piece of pithy quotations, titled *Just Call Me Fred*. Throughout all three of these books are the kinds of stories and sayings that educator Howard Gardner of Harvard has called "stories of identity" because they convey values, promote morale, create role models, and inform readers of the organization's decision-making process. *Learning to Lead* is chock full of precisely these kinds of stories.

Stories are always going to be part of a company's daily routine. Officially or unofficially, in boardrooms and around the water cooler, stories will be told. Some will show the company and its leaders in a favorable light, while others will be unflattering and even embarrassing. Positively or negatively, they all teach. For management, as Earl Holton and the Meijer family know, the key is to create an environment in which people speak openly and honestly about the company's strengths and weaknesses. "Stories aren't a distraction from work," said Thomas A. Stewart in a recent *Fortune* magazine article, "They're part of the fabric of it."

These are, however, more than just stories about Earl Holton. His book is also an important addition to Grand Rapids history. At a time when the community and its economy are booming, many commentators seek to understand that success. They can find many of their answers in Earl's comments about Meijer, its history, and operations.

Important, too, is his statement of the necessity for a locally owned company to participate in community organizations and events. Much is made about West Michigan's quality of life, including the support given social service and cultural organizations. Locally owned companies, Earl says, are more likely to support their community because doing so directly benefits their companies, employees, and customers. It is a simple concept, but one well worth remembering.

Whether your interest is Grand Rapids history, business management generally, or Meijer specifically, *Learning to Lead* has something to offer. Earl Holton tells a good story.

CHRONOLOGY

EARL HOLTON
Leading the Way
46 YEARS OF EXCELLENCE

1952
★ Bagger/Clerk
Cedar Springs (MI) Store

1955-1959
Store Manager

1960

1960
District Manager

1959
12 Stores

1961
First Thrifty Acres
Operations Manager

"Performance will
continue to outsell
promises"

1966
Vice President
Operations

m MEIJER
thrifty acres
SUPER MARKETS

1969
24 Stores

1970

"Go givers will be the
best go getters"

1977
Scanner Technology

1973
Senior Vice President,
Assistant General Manager

1975
Executive
Vice President

1980

1979
34 Stores

1984
50 Thrifty Years

1980
President
of Meijer

1981
Ohio

24 HOURS

"Where work is a pleasure,
life is a joy; have fun!"

1988
Open 24
Hours

Only the
best
MEIJER

1989
Only the
Best!

1989
68 Stores

1990

"Good Idea!"
Team Member Suggestion Program

1994
"Good Ideas!"

1994
Indiana

1995
Illinois

1998
79,000 Team Members
118 stores

1995
Our 100th store

THANKS EARL, FOR KEEPING
MEIJER ON THE PATH TO SUCCESS.

MEIJER Fresh

1998
Kentucky

Earl
Holton

Hank
Meijer

Fred
Meijer

Mark
Meijer

Lena
Meijer

Doug
Meijer

MEIJER

1

EARLY LESSONS:
1934-1952

MORE KIDS THAN BEDROOMS

I was born on January 23, 1934, in the heart of the Great Depression, in Manton, Michigan, where my dad was a minister for the Free Methodist Church. I was the sixth of seven kids. The baby of the family, my younger brother Paul, came along seven years later. The parsonages where

we lived never had enough bedrooms for our large family. I have an older sister named Lois who has kept our family together since my parents died. She's the one who keeps us all communicating, and I respect her a great deal for that. My sister Glenna and I are the closest in age, only two years apart. We became

The Holton family. Front row (l-r): Lois, Vera, Paul, Peter. Back row (l-r): Earl, Glenna, Jean, Mike, Keith

a two-person island in our family and have remained special friends.

ONE GENERATION REMOVED FROM ILLITERACY

My parents, Peter A. Holton and Vera Blanche Wilcox, both grew up in rural Sault Ste. Marie, Michigan, and their parents were farmers from Canada. My maternal grandfather, Abe Wilcox, had a dairy farm and a well-kept secret. I was in my thirties when I happened to ask my parents, "How come Grandma always read the Bible to Grandpa, but Grandpa never read the Bible to Grandma?" Very embarrassed, my mother finally said, "Your grandfather couldn't read." Then I realized I was only one generation removed from illiteracy, and that my

Vera and Peter Holton

grandfather's illiteracy had probably spurred my mother to pass on a love of reading to me.

Perhaps because of my mother's interest in books, I developed varied reading interests. Depending on my mood, I read everything from history and biographies to mysteries. One book that has had a strong impact on me is *Ladies' Paradise*, written by Emile Zola. Despite its peculiar name, the book is about Bon Marché, the first great department store in Paris. The book gives a detailed description of Bon Marché, the entrepreneur who built it up, and its impact on the small shopkeepers competing with it. I discovered the book through Hendrik Meijer. He read it as a young man in the Netherlands and it affected his thinking about retailing, the treatment of workers, and even competitors. Mr. Meijer's appreciation of that book helped me realize the insights that can be gained from all types of books.

MOVING DAYS

T he Free Methodist Church had a rule that its ministers could spend no more than four years at any one church, and it was not uncommon to be moved after three. I was born the second year my dad was in Manton, and after the third year we moved to the north side of Grand Rapids. We were there four years, and I started school at Leonard Street Elementary School.

In 1940, we moved to Cedar Springs. Due to a scheduling quirk, I was moved ahead half a year, putting me academically a full year ahead of my age group. By 1943, I had finished the second, third, and fourth grades in Cedar Springs, and the church moved us again, this time to Big Rapids.

Earl, just starting elementary school

I remember our four Big Rapids years as fantastic ones. My father had a successful church, one of the largest in the

Earl, in middle school

conference, and there was less need than previously for him to supplement his income with outside work. We lived in a nice house in a pleasant, middle class neighborhood, three blocks from the elementary school where I attended fifth and sixth grades.

Living across the street from a Catholic convent, school, and church gave me the opportunity to develop a new sense of the kindness and friendliness of these neighbors. I remember playing softball in a vacant lot next to the convent and breaking a window. I had seen those women in black clothing, but didn't know much about them, and thought, "Oh, boy, I'm in trouble." One of the nuns came out with the ball and said, "I bet you'd like to have this back." I said, "I'll go see my mama, and I'm sure she'll pay for the window." She said, "Don't you worry about it." I was greatly relieved.

In the spring, suckers ran in the section of the Muskegon River that meandered through town, and we'd catch and sell them for ten cents apiece. We thought we were pretty sharp, catching fish and selling them for a little spending money. Now, of course, I wonder how many of those people bought the fish to humor us and didn't really want a sucker for dinner at all.

Two of my buddies in Big Rapids were Bob and Carl Hull, who lived across the alley from us. Bob was a couple of years older than I was, and Carl was my age. Occasionally we would push their dad's car out of the garage into the alley, down to the street, and then start it up and go for a joyride. We'd bring it back and push it up the alley and into the garage. We were always sure Mr. Hull didn't know what we had done, but now, having raised my own family, I'm not so certain.

By the summer of 1947, I had finished the seventh and

eighth grades, and another moving day was looming. The church owned a campground in Manton, and every year we'd go there for two weeks of evangelical services and business meetings. Each family that wanted to stay on the grounds had a tent. Ours was about 12 by 16 feet, with a wooden floor and a little wooden kitchen annex, probably four by eight feet, which we locked our stuff in and boarded up until the next year. As a kid, I enjoyed these trips. It was a fun experience, kind of like going camping with my family.

Earl, at the Manton campground

As I got older, however, one aspect of camp bothered me more and more. The district superintendents would meet during the conference and decide where each minister was going, based on criteria that I didn't know and couldn't understand. All I knew was that if you had been in the same church for three or four years, you had to move. The hardest part was how you found out if and where you were moving. On Saturday afternoon, around four or five o'clock, after the business session was done, the bishop read the appointments for the next year. I stood in line with everybody else to discover where I was going to live. I felt that the situation could have been handled differently. As a result, I've always tried to give every consideration to family concerns when Meijer needs to move team members to new locations.

Manton campground assembly hall

After the summer meeting you went immediately to your new church. When I was a teenager in 1948, this meant leaving Big Rapids and moving to Greenville. It would have been a lot easier to make that move if the church had given some explanation. As it was, my father went from one of the two or three wealthiest churches in the conference to one of the smallest and poorest. I think the church officials hoped he would be able to expand its membership.

The new church was a small structure without an entry or foyer, just a cement block building with one room, the chapel. Sunday school attendance was only 26. It was a difficult situation, a small congregation in a very low-income neighborhood. The congregation members were good, hard-working people, and I made some good friends, but Dad was paid only $25 a week, plus three extra dollars to tend the furnace and clean the building. The church didn't even have indoor plumbing. There were outhouses behind our garage, but many members expected to use the toilet in the parsonage. My mother didn't cotton to that much.

One of Rev. Holton's first churches

To make ends meet, my father worked outside the home, doing painting and decorating. In his second year, the congregation offered to raise his pay to $30 if he would stop his other work, but with a daughter in college and two sons still at home, he couldn't afford to accept their offer. After three years in Greenville, he decided to leave the ministry and ended up managing an apple orchard and some oil wells, which he absolutely loved. Being outdoors with nature always gave him a good feeling.

YOUR COACH NEEDS YOU

I had a heavy school load in ninth grade, but I did moderately well except for Latin with Miss Burns, who quickly recognized that I needed glasses. She called me up to her desk one day and said, "Do you have good vision?"

I said, "Yeah, sure."

"Okay," she said, "I've got this stuff on the board. Why don't you sit in the back row where you've been sitting and tell me what it says?" So I stumbled through it. "Now sit in the front row and tell me what it says." I read it easily. She said, "I think you better tell your parents you need your vision checked."

It wasn't an especially memorable incident, but it did help me realize that there are many people like me who are reluctant to ask for help, and it is important to be observant to see those needs and offer assistance. Miss Burns did me a real favor.

After one year, I dropped Latin in favor of geography, which was taught by football and baseball coach John Heinzelman, one of a very small number of people who really had a special impact on my life. I was in geography for only a few days when he called me up to his desk after class.

Coach Heinzelman

"Are you in athletics?"

"No."

"Why not?"

"Got a hernia."

"Had it long?"

"Yes, since I was three."

"Well, that's a problem. I want to see you in my office after your last class." He never said "please," "thank you," or anything else, just "be in my office after your last class."

When I got there, he said, "I think you need some goals. You can't play football, but you're our new football manager. You'll be assistant manager this year, and next year you'll be our football manager. I want you to be manager of the baseball team, too." He never asked me if I wanted to or not. It wasn't a punishment, it was an order. His intervention turned

> *He never asked me if I wanted to or not. It wasn't a punishment, it was an order. His intervention turned my life around.*

my life around. Thanks to him, I started running with kids who were studying and looking toward college and careers, and I learned what it meant to be goal-oriented. Many years later I told this story to my friend Dick Gillett, who asked if I had ever thanked John Heinzelman for his encouragement. That got me thinking, and I wrote a letter of appreciation that reached Coach Heinzelman at his Florida retirement home shortly before he died. I'm glad I wrote that letter.

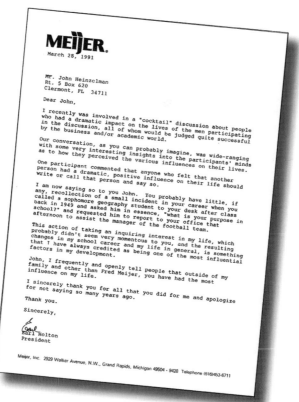

Earl's letter to Coach Heinzelman

BACK IN CEDAR SPRINGS

Before I began my senior year in high school, we moved back to Cedar Springs and Dad started building a house of our own. We had very little money — you don't worry about your investments a whole lot at $25 a week — but somehow my parents had managed to save up two hundred and some dollars. So we dug the basement with a horse and a drag line. Then Dad laid up all the blocks and built the house. It wasn't big, and it wasn't finished — he had sheetrock on one side of the joists and a subfloor when we moved in August — but it was ours.

One of the first things I did when we returned to Cedar Springs was renew my friendship with Gordy Doyle, who had been my best friend when we lived there earlier. He was president of the senior class and

Cedar Springs High School drama club.
Earl, on right arm of sofa.
Gordy Doyle, on left arm of sofa

captain of the football squad, and as soon as he heard I was moving back, he came to see me and asked if I could play football.

"No, I can't," I said.

"Why not?"

"I've got a hernia."

My older brother Mike also lived in Cedar Springs, where he had started a plumbing and propane gas business. I worked for him during the summer, and it wasn't more than a couple of days later that the football coach showed up at Mike's store and introduced himself. Then he said, "Gordon Doyle tells me you can't play football. Why not?"

"I have a hernia."

"Did you ever play football?"

"Yes, in the eighth grade."

"How'd you play your football then?"

"I don't know. I guess they didn't see the hernia when I went for my physical."

"Well, let's try it here," he said.

I passed the physical with flying colors and became part of the football team, where I ended up being one of the heaviest kids on the squad.

Earl, as a linebacker in Cedar Springs

My stint in Greenville as team manager gave me the confidence to go out for football in Cedar Springs. Being part of the team also made it easier to become acquainted with both students and teachers in my new school. I made several friends and met my wife-to-be.

MIKE, MY BROTHER AND MY BOSS

My brother Mike put me on the payroll of his fledgling plumbing and propane gas business while I was in high school in Greenville. Although I don't think he needed my help all that badly, I worked on Saturdays, and he picked me up in Greenville, drove me to Cedar Springs, and brought me home every week until I got a car of my own. To help me earn more money, he hired me to make the bases for the propane tanks he sold. I

Holton Plumbing & LP Gas

11

had forms, and I'd mix the concrete and set bolts into the bases during the week. He'd pay me a flat rate for each one and pick them up when he picked me up on Saturdays. That way he could legitimately pay me for something, instead of simply giving me the money. I think it made us both feel better. It's the kind of lesson about giving people a hand instead of a handout that you take with you the rest of your life.

On my sixteenth birthday I bought a car, a beat-up 1936 Ford. Almost every Saturday when I drove to Cedar Springs, Mike would take my car across the street to the local mechanic and have minor repairs made to keep it running. All I had to do was buy the gas. I remember one Friday night I was driving around with some friends. We got to roughhousing and the driver's seat broke loose. I rode to work the next day sitting on a potato crate. While I was working, the car disappeared for awhile and returned with the seat welded back in place.

DONNALEE

Mike and I often ate lunch, and sometimes supper, at the Cedar Cafe, where a vivacious, high-energy young woman named Donnalee Engel worked as a waitress. Although she would later become my wife, she saw me then as more of a nuisance than potential boyfriend because Mike and I tended to talk well beyond the cafe's eight o'clock closing time. I didn't learn until much, much later, after we were married, that Donnalee had dates on those nights and couldn't leave until we did.

Donnalee

Donnalee and I didn't start dating until the football season ended. Then I asked her for a date to a basketball game, but she was working. I said, "Well, I'll meet you in the bleachers." Ever since, she's needled me about not wanting to pay for her ticket. So I've tried to buy enough tickets to make up for that.

The Cedar Cafe, c. 1950

We were married in August of 1952, shortly after she graduated from high school, and moved into an apartment in Cedar Springs.

I think we were the last couple in Cedar Springs to be shivareed. Today, few people have heard the term or know what it means, but at one time it was a way for rural communities to have a party and welcome a newly married couple. My brothers and brothers-in-law were behind the affair. They came banging on pots and pans, got us out of bed, put us in the back of my brother's three-quarter-ton Dodge truck, and drove us up and down Main Street. I was in my pajamas and Donnalee was in her nightgown, and they threatened to drop one of us off at one end of the street and the other one at the other end. They also took the wrapping paper from our wedding presents, which I had carefully bagged, and shredded and spread it all over our apartment. Throughout the whole affair, they made quite a racket, and our landlord was not happy. We moved not too long after that.

As I look back over more than 46 years, I can't over-emphasize the importance of the role Donnalee has played in our life together. She is a great listener and adviser who has provided strong support, tremendous empathy, and, occasionally, some sympathy. When I worked in the stores, my schedule included Saturdays and evenings. I knew from her actions and conversations that my Saturday evening absences were especially difficult, but she never complained. In addition to doing a phenomenal job raising our four children, she then went on to develop her own career as a volunteer for several community organizations.

FIVE WEEKS ON THE ASSEMBLY LINE

After graduating from high school in 1952, I considered going to college. My parents sat down with me one evening and asked me about my plans. I said I thought I'd like to go to college, and I'd visited Davenport Business College and Grand Rapids Junior College. Although my parents assured me they would do everything they could to help me, Dad had fallen and broken his back the previous October and they didn't have any money. I didn't have any money either. I didn't know how I could pay bills, drive to Grand Rapids, go to school, and buy books when none of us had any money. So instead, I decided to get a job.

Earl, as a senior in high school

I was seventeen when I graduated, and I went to work full time for my brother. Mike and I worked together on plumbing jobs and propane deliveries, and I did the daily bookkeeping and took care of the store. At that time, Mike was trying to build a business with no capital, but he took the time to provide me with a good start in the business world.

That winter, business was extremely slow. There were three of us: Mike, a man named Jim Haynes, and me. I was writing the paychecks, and I knew that when I wrote them on Saturday, I could cash mine on Monday or Tuesday or Wednesday, but by the end of the week Mike would often be out of money. So he and I had a heart-to-heart talk and agreed he couldn't afford both Jim and me. It wasn't easy for me to go out looking for another job, but I felt I was making the best decision for Mike and his business.

I had heard Continental Motors in Muskegon was hiring, and I landed a job in the shipping department. I had just turned eighteen, and although the pay was good and the work was easy, I spent the next five weeks in total misery. I knew immediately I could never, ever spend a lifetime doing that work. Continental Motors had prospered during World War II, and the company was still doing very well. There were a lot of workers with not a lot to do. When they reached their quotas, they sat around playing cards and washed up early to leave at the end of the day. I felt I was being paid to work, and didn't go along. I couldn't stand it. I'd walk in, turn my brain off, and leave it off until I left. Finally, I went to the foreman and said, "I'll be leaving Friday."

He said, "Did you get another job?"

"No."

"What are you going to do?"

"I have no idea, but I'm not going to do this."

I went back to Mike and told him what I had done, and he said, "Gosh, I'd like to have you come back but I can't afford you." The best he could offer was a commission if I wanted to go out and sell stoves and other propane-fueled appliances door-to-door. Well, I don't have the personality for selling appliances cold turkey like that, and I proved it. Over the next couple of months, I didn't sell enough appliances to do him or me any good.

Earl, as a young man

Fortunately, spring was coming and he had a plumbing job open up, so I went back to work for him and worked through the summer and into the fall. By December, however, I saw the same thing coming again. That's when I told Mike I was going to take the day off and try again to find another job.

CHAPTER 2

LEARNING THE
MEIJER WAY:
1952-1959

I DON'T KNOW BEANS FROM CARROTS

As I walked down Main Street that December day, I didn't know what I was looking for, and I certainly didn't expect to start a lifelong career, but that is what happened.

Cedar Springs Meijer store, c. 1950

Walking by the Meijer supermarket in Cedar Springs, I stopped in on an impulse and asked Cecil McKinnon, the store manager, if he had any openings. As fate would have it, the Korean War created a shortage of help. His two full-time clerks had received their draft notices and he needed someone immediately. In those days, the hiring was done in Grand Rapids, and McKinnon sent me to the Meijer main office at Michigan and Fuller. I was interviewed by Jack Van Overloop and several others, including Pat Jameson and Harry Grashoff, who was the personnel manager. They said, "Well, we'll put you to work."

A Meijer produce area, c. 1952

I also met Hendrik Meijer during one of the interviews. I remember telling him, "I don't know beans from carrots, Mr. Meijer."

"That's all right," he said. "We'll teach you."

Somehow or other we got to talking about the Dutch nationality, and I said, "Well, fortunately, I do have a little Dutch blood in me — some Pennsylvania Dutch."

19

He started laughing. "That's German, so it doesn't qualify. But we'll give you Dutch shots and you'll be okay." Once in a while I tell the Meijer leadership classes that I'm still taking Dutch shots after 46 years.

I started working at Meijer on December 22, 1952, and my first pay rate was $1.16 per hour — Mike had been paying me $1.25 an hour. Many years later, I mentioned that to Mr. Meijer. "You know, I always figured you could have paid me a dollar and a quarter if you hadn't had so many people spend their time interviewing me."

Earl and Donnalee, c. 1953

Working at Meijer was a good, steady job, but even with a raise, my paycheck barely stretched from payday to payday. Donnalee became pregnant during our first year of marriage and she worked at Wolverine as a secretary to help put aside some money to pay for the baby. Wolverine had a rule that when you were six months pregnant, you had to leave your job. I recall one evening while Donnalee was pregnant, we went out for a ride in our '47 Pontiac and stopped at Hough's Dairy Bar to get ice cream cones. As I pulled the change out of my pocket, I realized I didn't have enough money for two cones. We went home empty-handed, and I made up my mind I'd never be in that position again. I picked the right employer, for if I ever need an ice cream cone, I'll ask Fred for a card for a free cone from the Purple Cow.

I enjoyed working at Meijer and liked the grocery business right from the beginning. Even though my brother Mike offered me a chance to come back to work for him, I decided to stay. I will always appreciate the start that Mike gave me in the business world. Later on, his business began to thrive, and he eventually became one of the largest propane dealers in the Midwest. I will never forget how he kept me on his payroll even when he couldn't afford it.

NO USE CRYING OVER SPILT MILK

One of the first things I learned at the Cedar Springs store was how to stock the bread shelves. The bread came in wooden nesting boxes, and my whole approach was to show how quickly and efficiently I could get it on the shelves. After a short time, I had gotten the process to the point where I could bring in more boxes of bread at one time than anyone else and stock them faster. So there I was, wheeling the bread boxes out of the store as fast as I could. There were no automatic doors in those days, just a wood frame door with a lot of glass so people could see through and not crash into each other. I pushed the door open with the breadbox, but I had it tilted up too far and I hit the glass. Before I had a notion of what was happening, all the glass in the door shattered.

I cleaned up that mess and spent the next few hours bagging. Then Cecil, the manager told me to fill the milk case. The usual procedure was to put four wire baskets of milk cartons on a two-wheeled cart and take it to the case. Unfortunately, I had not learned my lesson that morning and figured I could make up for my earlier mistake by putting an additional couple of baskets on my cart. You can guess what happened next. Just as I was passing a large group of women waiting for service at the meat counter, the six cartons buckled in the middle and spilled all

Busy aisles of a Meijer supermarket

over the floor. There went my 50 percent increase in productivity.

I got my second mess of the day cleaned up, filled the milk case the proper way, and then went up front, took my apron off, and punched out. Cecil saw me and asked, "What are you doing?"

I said, "I've never been fired yet, and you're not going to be the first one to do it."

"Get your apron on. You're not leaving."

I don't know why he kept me on; maybe with the shortage of help he didn't have any choice. Maybe he needed a warm body. Whatever his reason, it impressed me that he did not fire me, and I vowed to take advantage of my second chance. I think this reinforces the old saying, "It doesn't matter how many pails of milk you spill, just don't lose the cow."

I've used that lesson in our leadership classes. I talk about not being too harsh with people who make mistakes. Don't write them up for everything they do wrong. Don't get ready to fire a team member who makes two mistakes the same day. There's a time when you figuratively put your arm around the person's shoulders and say, "I wish I could have prevented that from happening to you." Maybe

> *There's a time when you figuratively put your arm around the person's shoulders and say, "I wish I could have prevented that from happening to you." . . . that's what Fred has done with me for many years.*

that's part of what Cecil was doing, and, of course, that's what Fred has done with me for many years.

Right from the beginning, working at Meijer was a very positive experience. We were a small company, and when Fred and Mr. Meijer (we always called Hendrik Meijer "Mr.

Meijer" and Fred Meijer simply "Fred") came into the store, they talked to everyone. I met both of them my first week on the job. They may or may not have remembered my name, but I knew them and they knew me. The climate was a very positive human environment. I made many missteps along the way, but the culture they had created respected all team members and encouraged us to give quality service to our guests. It was a culture that I liked.

YOU CAN'T DO BUSINESS FROM AN EMPTY WAGON

I started at Cedar Springs as a general clerk. In addition to stocking bread and milk, I learned how to change prices on canned goods. In those days, we stamped the price on each product and then changed it if necessary. It was the most basic job in the business, and that's where I started. We used nail polish remover and a rag or steel wool to wipe off the old price, and then we'd restamp it. It wasn't fun or challenging, but it had to be done.

An early Meijer delivery truck

After I'd been with the store awhile, I took my turn in the storeroom. The weekly delivery came in on Tuesday, and as the goods came off the conveyor from the truck, we would move them into their places in the storeroom. The farther back in the storeroom we got, the more walking we'd have to do.

Once we had the goods organized, we would stock the shelves. That meant cutting the top off each case, marking the price, and wheeling the cases out to the floor, where cashiers would put them on the shelves whenever they weren't busy. Sometimes, the aisles became so jammed with merchandise that shopping became almost impossible. By Thursday night, we would have the aisles all cleared.

The cardboard boxes from each shipment went into the storeroom. If you needed something from the storeroom, you had to climb over the cardboard to get it and then crawl back. We burned the cardboard once a week. One time, I built the fire a little too big, and the sparks almost burned down the neighbor's house, but that's another story.

I thought the system of marking the product in the storeroom was inefficient and could be done by one person instead of two. I had a chance to prove that I could do it better and faster when the person in charge of the storeroom was out sick. But when the storeroom manager returned, Cecil never corrected the problem. He knew the solution was there and he knew who had found it, he just wasn't going to change the people or the system. That's when I first realized that although you can find ways to make things better and more efficient, the trick is persuading others to make the change.

That's when I first realized that although you can find ways to make things better and more efficient, the trick is persuading others to make the change.

Meijer was a growing company, with many opportunities for advancement, so it wasn't long before I got my first promotion to assistant manager at Cedar Springs. I was still a pretty young guy at this point, and it was kind of exciting to go from an hourly wage to a salary.

I had been with the company less than a year when I was transferred to the Greenville store as assistant manager. Two weeks after I arrived, the store manager was replaced. Not only had he done a poor

Greenville Meijer store

job of stocking products, he was always late for work and took long lunches. I remember Mr. Meijer telling him that you can't do business from an empty wagon, and the Greenville store wagon was empty. The new manager, Harry Church, organized the work and filled the shelves. Harry was good to work for. He had a good sense of human relations and helped me learn how to motivate people to do things because they wanted to.

WE DON'T CUT CHICKENS THAT WAY

Donnalee and I continued to live in Cedar Springs while I worked in Greenville. When an opportunity arrived, I asked to be transferred back to Cedar Springs.

At the time, Meijer's meat department operated separately from the rest of the store, because meat had to be bought, stocked, and marketed differently. In those days, meat managers were pretty much autonomous. They had their own break rooms and their own coffeepots. It was a separate world that went back to the days when grocery stores did not automatically include meat departments. Meijer's earliest meat

An early Meijer meat department

departments tended to be leased operations on the theory that they were different, and a grocer wouldn't know how to run them anyway.

Not long after I returned to Cedar Springs, I tangled with the meat manager over a potentially large order from a popular restaurant up the road in Sand Lake called the Steer Haus. One day, the owner of the restaurant asked us to cut his chicken orders a certain way. The meat manager told him, "We don't cut chickens that way." I couldn't figure out what difference it made. I thought we should cut them any way he wanted. The Cedar Springs store had a low volume of sales and was struggling to make money, and here we were losing a big customer because we wouldn't cut chickens the way he wanted.

It bothered me to lose business then, and it still does today. So I started complaining. But I was lower on the managerial totem pole than the meat manager, and it was not smart for assistant managers to complain about a meat manager.

I went to the store manager first, who was nominally responsible for the meat department. But he wasn't interested in rocking the boat, so I took my complaint to the district manager. I knew I was in trouble when he came to the store one day and took me for coffee across the street. Noting that "we obviously have a personality conflict between you and the meat manager," he announced that I was being sent to work at the Meijer store in Grand Rapids at Michigan and Fuller starting the next Monday. At that point, I really didn't think my future at Meijer was too bright.

LEARNING TO BE VISIBLE

The store manager at Michigan-Fuller was Louis (Bud) Clark, and although I would never hold him up as a model manager, I learned from him nonetheless. Bud would place his stock orders without checking the shelves, he played favorites among sales representatives and overstocked their items, and he made false refund slips to balance his books. But he also knew how to manage his workforce. One thing he taught me that I have never forgotten is the importance of being a

He said if you want to keep the carryout crew from loitering in the parking lot . . . all you need to do is occasionally take a stroll through the lot.

visible manager. He said that if you want to keep the carryout crew from loitering in the parking lot, or reduce other disciplinary problems, all you need to do is occasionally take a stroll through the lot, unannounced. Later, when I got my own store, I tried it, and it worked. I have been a firm believer in visible management ever since.

MEIJER TOWN FOODS

About five weeks after I reported for work at the Michigan-Fuller store, the manager's position opened up at the downtown store on Ottawa Street, known as Meijer Town Foods. Despite my recent demotion, Don Magoon, Fred's brother-in-law, and Joe Dotzauer, my district manager, encouraged me to apply. I didn't, but I was given the job anyway.

The store hadn't been open too long when I took over, and it was a tough store to operate. Although our guest count was high, the store had a low volume of sales. We would get busy at lunchtime and sell a whole lot of apples, soft

Meijer Town Foods, 1955

drinks, and bags of chips, but when the noon rush was over, business was slow until four or four thirty. After a second flurry of activity, we closed early. To turn a profit, we had to charge higher prices and offer a limited selection, and that was contrary to our commitment to have the same stock and prices in all stores.

Meijer has always offered a liberal return policy, and I learned early on that a few people will go to remarkable lengths to take advantage of that policy. I can remember a woman who asked for a refund on a watermelon although all that was left was the rind. She got her refund.

A REBEL IN STANDALE

I managed Meijer Town Foods for just six months before I was asked to go to Standale, on the western edge of Grand Rapids, and set up the new store Fred and his dad were opening in August 1955. One of my experiences there, like the chicken incident of the year before, confirmed my belief that a large organization has to make room for people who challenge the accepted way of doing things. Again, the rebel was me.

Earl, in Standale, c. 1955

At that time, we called the general merchandise departments in our supermarkets "home centers." It was the Christmas season and business was slower than I had hoped. A guest wanted an electric fry pan in a size that we did not have on display. I thought there might be one in the home center storeroom, but the director of home centers had concluded that store managers weren't to be trusted with keys to the home center storerooms. That policy was a burr under my saddle, but my protests to the district manager had gone nowhere.

Although I didn't have the key, I was determined to serve the guest. So I used a screwdriver to take the hinges off the door. Once I had found the right pan and made the sale, I put the hinges back on. I confessed to the breaking and entering the next morning, and I figured the incident would make an interesting addition to my personnel file. But Fred must have gotten wind of the situation, and instead of a reprimand, I got the keys.

I hope we always remain a company that has the flexibility to change the policy rather than punish initiative. That's why I have challenged our senior officers to make room for the rebel, to pay attention to the maverick who has good ideas but can't get through the bureaucracy. Too often, when team members don't conform, they are made to feel uncomfortable, and they leave. But there has to be room for the

I hope we always remain a company that has the flexibility to change the policy rather than punish initiative . . . to make room for the rebel . . . to pay attention to the maverick . . .

freethinker who may very well have that next great idea. Mining the employee resource lode is one of the keys to a successful business.

I'M NOT SURE ABOUT EARL'S FUTURE

I got to know Fred Meijer and his father early in my career. With a small company and only a few stores to visit, they came around to each store fairly often to see what was going on and to talk to their team members. While Mr. Meijer walked around the store doing his thing, Fred chatted about operational issues like sales and labor costs, wanting to know "What are you doing on this?" and "How are things going, do you need anything?"

At some point, I must have come to their attention. Certainly, by the time I got to Standale, I had become part of the team member group that was known on a first name basis, although that may not always have been a good thing. Many years later, I learned that Fred had initial reservations about my managerial potential. One day, he and his father

drove into the parking lot while I was going to the bank to make a deposit. I was walking because it gave me a chance to light up my pipe and get it rolling. At that time, the store was not doing much business. We were losing money, and there I

The Standale Meijer store, 1955

29

was "strolling" across the parking lot, as Fred put it. "Look at that, Dad," he said. "I don't think Earl will ever amount to a whole lot." Fortunately, he gave me plenty of opportunities to prove otherwise.

WE'VE GOT A PROBLEM

I learned a valuable lesson in leadership while I was at the Standale store. In those days, because the surrounding area was not yet built up, Standale was one of Meijer's smaller-volume operations, which meant we had the worst delivery schedule. Although the store was supposed to be stocked for the week by Tuesday afternoon, our delivery order did not arrive until the following day. Nevertheless, the supervisor was on my back. So I started ordering ahead of time, but that meant my back room was full over the weekend, and the requirement was that the back room

Standale Meijer Store

had to be empty on Saturday night. I decided my first goal was to take care of our guests by having goods on the shelves, and then I'd worry about the supervisor.

When we couldn't work out our differences, he announced that I had been placed on probation. That night, I called a store meeting and let the staff know what had happened. We stuck to our guns and continued to order early to keep our shelves stocked.

Two weeks later, the supervisor took me off probation. Shortly after that, he informed me I was getting a raise. I just looked at him and said, "How can I be so bad and so good at the same time?"

Since then, I've told our management time and time again, don't put team members on probation. Take care of problems as they arise, but don't make them sweat it out, wondering whether or not they have a job. That's not fair. It's like disciplinary layoffs that go beyond one or two days. After the initial period, the disciplinary value is lost and all that is left is bitterness. Discipline is one thing, but keeping workers off the job for two weeks or two months hits them in the pocketbook, and that's not right.

FIRST THINGS FIRST

By the late 1950s, Fred Meijer and his dad operated nine stores, four of which weren't doing particularly well. The downtown Grand Rapids store had a high customer count and low sales. Standale had a low volume of sales because it was new. The newly opened Leonard Street store on the west side had problems because it had a downstairs storeroom, requiring more time and more labor to stock the shelves. Finally, the Eastern Avenue store was not profitable; for the first time in that store's history, a manager had put the store in the red.

I can remember a supervisor saying, "Hey, whatever you need for the store you can't have. We just don't have the budget." Despite the tight finances, however, feelings of fairness and attention to team members permeated this small company. The Meijer policy seemed to be,

The Meijer policy seemed to be, first we have to be able to pay the wages, and then we'll figure out how to take care of other things. I guess that's part of what I liked so much.

first we have to be able to pay the wages, and then we'll figure out how to take care of other things. I guess that's part of what I liked so much.

WHEN DO YOU WANT ME THERE?

I enjoyed working at the Standale store. It had a low volume of sales and was only eighteen months old, but I had all the systems working smoothly. For added personal convenience, I lived about ten minutes away. So when Joe Dotzauer approached me to manage the Eastern Avenue store, I said, "No thanks."

Joe reminded me that anyone can open a new store, but not everyone can take a problem store and

The neighborhood surrounding the Eastern Avenue Meijer store, 1956

make it work. I got the message and realized I was being given another chance to show what I could do, so I said, "When do you want me there?"

The Eastern Avenue store really was important in my career because the opportunity for change was so dramatic. The store was in bad shape. At the time I went there, it had a serious labor overage. In fact, the dollars spent on labor over the budget equaled the budget overages of the other eight stores put together. By working out better schedules and making procedures more efficient, I was able to see a change in short order, and profitability was restored.

The Eastern Avenue store was in an upper-middle-income neighborhood populated by young professionals and their families,

The Eastern Avenue Meijer store, 1956

who would later move to the suburbs. For some reason, guests requested a lot of refunds. I don't know if it was their expectation of high quality products and service or their conservative nature, but they did not hesitate to bring things back. Despite the refunds, the store soon had a good margin, and those guests taught me to stay on my toes all the time. That's an attitude I've tried to instill in all Meijer team members right down to the newest one.

DON'T GO THERE

One of the side benefits of my experience at the Eastern Avenue store was the opportunity to get to know Bob VanderArk, the grocery department manager. Bob subsequently left Meijer, but came back and now plays a key role in buying general merchandise. While I was still at the Eastern Avenue store, Joe Dotzauer encouraged me to apply for the newly available position of manager at the Michigan-Fuller store, the largest store in the company at the time and the headquarters for the entire Meijer operation. So I put my name in the hat, expecting to get the promotion. When someone I regarded as one of the weakest store managers was chosen instead, I let Joe have it.

The parking lot of the Michigan-Fuller Meijer store, c. 1956

"You just told me that I'm not as good as he is," I said. "You asked me to apply and the fact that you picked him means you think he's a better store manager than I am." I didn't buy Joe's lame excuses, and six months later, when the position opened again, I was transferred there.

My fellow store managers warned me, "Don't go there." They felt that such a high-volume store would be hard to run, and that I might get too many helpful suggestions because Mr. Meijer, Fred, and all the supervisors were so close by. In the other store managers' minds, whoever was running that store was under special scrutiny because all the windows of the second-floor main office looked out into the store.

Actually, I had less supervision at Michigan-Fuller than I ever had at any other store. But there were more people going through the store because the stairway to the office was at the back and the cafeteria was in the front. Every day, several times a day, the office staff walked down the aisle between frozen foods and coffee to go to work or take a break. If he was in the office, Mr. Meijer came down for his coffee too. I quickly learned to have that aisle looking good. It was so simple. I kept the whole store clean, but I

Earl (far left), with City Commissioner Carl Eschels and his wife, and Grand Rapids Mayor Christian Sonneveldt in the Michigan-Fuller cafeteria

made sure that aisle got a spit-and-polish going over every morning. The part of my store they saw always looked good.

It was also while I was at Michigan-Fuller that I developed my "whistling" strategy, another example of being a visible manager. My workforce included a large number of smokers, and they sometimes violated the rule banning smoking in the storeroom. Otherwise, they were good workers and I didn't want to discipline them too severely. So I developed the habit of whistling a tune as I approached the storeroom. Sure enough, there was never a cigarette to be found. Thanks to my whistling, they were careful with their smoking, and I could save any disciplinary steps for more serious offenses. Although we never talked about it, I'm sure they knew I whistled to let them know I was in the area, just as I knew they were having an occasional cigarette.

ALL THAT POWER AND VERY FEW FREINDS

It was also while I was at Michigan-Fuller that I met one of Grand Rapids' most powerful figures, Frank McKay. He had been a force in Michigan politics for many years, and although he was getting older, the state's most influential leaders still responded to his call.

I had first become aware of his influence while I was at Standale, where he owned a great deal of property and had sold the Meijers their store site. I was having trouble applying for a beer and wine license until I happened to mention McKay's name. Then the license was approved with no more questions.

At Michigan-Fuller, Mr. McKay would often summon me to have a cup of coffee when he came in to shop. He would tell me stories about his days in politics and his various properties and investments, including a hotel in Florida. He was unable to trust people. Everyone, it seemed, was taking advantage of him, and he believed that many of his employees were stealing from him. He had been a tough wheeler and dealer when he was younger, and now it seemed he had few friends he could trust. I enjoyed my conversations with Mr. McKay, but as I observed his loneliness and suspicion, I knew that I wanted to conduct my own life in such a way that I could look back more happily than he did.

AM I WASTING YOUR TIME?

In sharp contrast were my conversations with Hendrik Meijer. Although I had met Mr. Meijer on his visits to my other stores, I did not really get to know him until I managed Michigan-Fuller. Extremely well dressed, very tall, and with an erect military carriage, he was an imposing figure and, from my perspective, a little awesome to approach.

It was not uncommon for him to come from the corporate office and invite me to join him for coffee. I don't know whether he singled me out or if it was just his method of operation. Either way, it was a very valuable experience. I remember sitting in the cafeteria one day when he pointed out that the team member at the cash register was stealing. I was sure I knew better, and I refused to believe him (at least until I caught her).

Hendrik Meijer

From then on I followed his advice to "watch the cash register." Essentially he was telling me, "Pay attention. Watch what's going on." It's an important lesson that I still try to teach in the stores today.

Essentially he was telling me, "Pay attention. Watch what's going on." It's an important lesson that I still try to teach in the stores today.

Often when we had coffee, Mr. Meijer talked about his past and his life experiences. The conversations sometimes continued back at the office. Once, after the offices had been moved to the basement, he was seated across from my desk relating some past experiences. Playing the part of a young, ambitious executive, I started shuffling some papers. He stopped talking, looked at me, and said, "Am I wasting your time?"

"No, Mr. Meijer. You're not wasting my time."

"Well, I don't mean to. The only reason I tell you these old stories is maybe I can help you avoid making some of the same mistakes I made." I was never again too busy to listen to him.

On September 7, 1962, we had a fire at Michigan-Fuller. A would-be burglar had stolen a welding torch from the gas station across the street and broken into the store intending to open the safe. But when he lit the torch, there was an explosion that burned down the store, and he ran away empty-handed. Even if he had succeeded in cracking the safe, he'd have gotten only $200; we didn't keep much money in the safe overnight.

As Mr. Meijer and I stood outside surveying the damage, I was eager to get busy. He suggested coffee instead. "Earl, there isn't anything you can change right now. Let's go get a cup of coffee and we can chat. Then we'll get started on what has to be done." He was right, and it was another lesson learned. He was a good teacher, and he gave me a wealth of knowledge.

3

MOVING TO THE
FRONT OFFICE:
1959-1966

I'M TALKING ABOUT YOUR BEHAVIOR

By 1959, I had been a Meijer store manager for four years, spending an average of a year at each of four stores. Although the Michigan-Fuller store was the company's largest operation, after a year I was beginning to get antsy. My systems were up and running and the work had become routine. In fact, I always had trouble with routine. I liked surprises and I thrived on new challenges. That's why rumors of a possible merger with the Plumb supermarket chain excited me.

The Michigan-Fuller Meijer store, c. 1959

I had no idea of the business benefits of a merger or what it might mean in terms of synergies or reduction of overhead. But I liked the idea that we would suddenly double in size, and I looked forward to the career opportunities a larger company could offer. We used to joke that if the merger went through, we'd be "plumb" crazy.

The merger negotiations turned out to have important implications for my future because I was one of two Meijer store managers under consideration for a district manager position with the new company. As a job candidate, I was tested and interviewed by an industrial psychologist. Even though the merger failed, the interview itself served me well from that day forward.

The psychologist began by saying, "I would guess that you have a pretty loyal crew, and that's all fine and dandy. But your behavior gets in the way when you first meet people. In a store, you work with people for an extended length of time and they get to know you. But people don't relate to you as well when they first meet you because you keep everything inside." When I told him, as my mother had often told me, that it was my personality, he said, "I'm not worried about your personality, Earl. I'm talking about your behavior."

Earl as a store manager, c. 1957

"Smile and look friendly," he said. "You can't just feel like you're a nice guy, you have to look like one, too." I took his advice to heart and immediately began walking through the store smiling at and greeting every single guest. I didn't always know them by name, but I knew them because they came in on regular days every week. It didn't take long before I really learned to enjoy greeting our guests. Later, when I left the stores and went to work in the office, I missed my contact with Meijer guests the most. I am still a reserved person, but that interview caused me to change my behavior. Today, being friendly to guests is something we encourage all Meijer team members to work on, even if their "personality" doesn't always make it easy.

> *That interview caused me to change my behavior. Today, being friendly to guests is something we encourage all Meijer team members to work on, even if their "personality" doesn't always make it easy.*

WHOM DO YOU SUGGEST WE PROMOTE?

It was also in 1959 that Fred concluded we had become top-heavy with supervisory personnel. We had candy specialists and personnel specialists and other specialists galore, all supervising their own departments in each store and overseeing the activities of the store managers. It got to be a joke that Meijer ought to buy a bus to bring the specialists around to the stores. Fred and his dad were trying to find the secrets to good store operations and growth in sales and profits, but they had been thinking ahead of our size, and they had added more specialists than we needed. So Fred decided to eliminate an entire management level by replacing specialists with a single operations director, Harvey Lemmen, the office manager.

Harvey brought a great deal of professionalism and stability to his new position, and he supervised all the stores for about six months. With 11 stores by then, and a party store, Fred and Mr. Meijer felt that Harvey had more area to cover than was reasonable to expect, so I was brought into the office as the company's only district manager.

Harvey Lemmen, c. 1962

At my first weekly management meeting, before I even had a chance to learn my new job, the Meijers announced that we were going to cut all prices in all stores. We were also going to get rid of our in-house trading stamps, which we called Goodwill stamps and which hadn't been terribly effective because we started late and stamps were beginning to lose their impact. Up to that point, Meijer had been a conventional small supermarket

Team members mark down prices

chain like others that sprang up after World War II. Now we were getting out of stamps and into discount. It was a great move. We got lots of attention, and our volume increased overnight.

Six months later, in September 1960, Harvey was called in to see Fred. When he came back to our shared office next to the chimney, he said, "Fred and his dad want to see you."

I didn't normally get called in to their office, so I wondered what was up. As soon as I sat down, Fred said, to my surprise, "Harvey's just taken the sales manager's job. Would you like to take Harvey's job?"

"You know I'm not ready," I said. I'd been moving very, very fast. "I'm twenty-six. I need to learn more about the business." I really believed that.

Fred said, "Okay. Who would you suggest we promote to be your boss?"

The idea of someone else getting the job didn't appeal to me either, so I quickly concluded that I was as ready as anyone. It was a good play on Fred's part to respond with that question instead of making some other statement. And so I was made operations director, with responsibility for warehousing, labor relations, personnel, and store supervision. I had a lot to learn, and it was all going to be on-the-job training.

HOW DID THEY DO THAT, EARL?

Our sales volume was growing at a phenomenal rate since we had gone discount, and our warehouse on Alpine Avenue in Grand Rapids couldn't keep products stocked and delivered to the stores. The warehouse manager had quit when I was promoted to district manager because he thought he should have gotten the job, and things were a mess. Instead of being two or three hours late with deliveries, we were running two or three days behind. Stores were out of stock, and poor inventory control meant we didn't know if we had certain items or not.

Being brand new to the job, I really didn't know how the system

Meijer's first warehouse on Alpine Avenue

should work, and I didn't know what to do. So I went to Fred and asked, "Is there somebody who can help me?" There was. A consultant named Dave Gardineer was an old pro. Just by looking around, he could accurately tell how much inventory a warehouse carried. With his help, I did what had to be done to organize the operation, rearrange the reserve inventory, and see that things ran on schedule.

Analyzing the problem at the time, I realized almost immediately that the warehouse guys were not to blame. They weren't prepared for the job, and that was our fault. I've always believed that if you put workers in a job they can't handle, you're the one who's made the mistake.

From that time on, I made up my mind we would have efficient warehouses even if they were old. With the wind whistling through the

Team members working in the Alpine Avenue warehouse

building, the warehouse on Alpine was so bad that in the wintertime people ate lunch in the cooler to warm up. The company made a significant investment in 1964, and we opened a brand new warehouse in Walker. We added on to the Walker warehouse a couple of times before building a second warehouse ten years later in Lansing.

I was also determined to update the equipment we used to haul products and merchandise. Our old, small semi-trailers were only 32 feet long, pulled by small Ford tractors. To replace them I wanted two used 40-footers. They had to be used because we couldn't afford new. We paid a third of the total in cash and the rest in due bills.

Once the trailers were painted and delivered, the warehouse crew loaded one up. That's when my troubles began. The truck wells at the warehouse were at a relatively steep angle, and our small Ford tractors didn't have enough power to pull out a fully-loaded trailer.

So there my new purchase sat. I had no choice but to get a bigger tractor and start upgrading the entire fleet. I tell this story as a lesson on the importance of carefully assessing all the factors before making an important decision. I should have known before making a purchase what size trailers our warehouse and tractors would accommodate.

A Meijer truck, 1965

My transport woes continued after we moved to our current headquarters in Walker in 1964. One day, the warehouse manager called me and said, "I don't know how to tell you this, boss, but somebody stole one of our semi-tractors." When I delivered the news to Fred, he looked at me and said, "How did they do that, Earl?"

Apparently, the keys to the tractors were not very specific in those days, and if you had a few keys, you could usually find one to fit any rig. Moreover, we didn't have much security. Someone simply came in and drove our tractor away. We never found it.

Even though the theft made Fred unhappy, he did not blame me. Instead, he chuckled at my discomfort and said, "Well, I guess we'll have to get another one, won't we? Tell me again how they did that, Earl."

That was Fred's way of handling problems. He always told me, "I don't like surprises. Keep me informed. Let me be part of your problem and its solution." More than once I heeded that advice, and it always served me well. Fred never shot the messenger.

THRIFTY ACRES

By the early 1960s, several large discount stores, including Miracle Mart, Arlan's, and Spartan-Atlantic Mills, had come to Grand Rapids. They were general merchandise retailers, but also sold some groceries. Although they stayed away from meat and fresh produce, we saw them as a threat. What concerned Fred and his father the most was that the discount stores might use financial incentives to attract supermarkets to operate in the same strips as they did, placing us at a competitive disadvantage. The Meijers' solution to the problem turned out to be a radically new concept in supermarket and retail merchandising.

Observing the high-volume traffic enjoyed by Miracle Mart, which operated next to our Plainfield Avenue store, Fred and Mr. Meijer concluded that they could join a discount store and a supermarket under one roof. They decided to build a large addition to the Grand Rapids store at Kalamazoo Avenue and 28th Street, and they named their new venture Thrifty Acres.

Construction of the first Meijer Thrifty Acres

The Meijers had invested a ton of money in construction for the new facility and were taking a tremendous gamble. The idea was that Meijer would own the building and operate the supermarket and health and beauty care (HBC) components. The other departments within the building would be leased to a variety of tenants. Two executives were brought in from New York, one to operate Thrifty Acres and the other to serve as discount store manager. Harvey Lemmen was in charge of sales, and, as operations director of Meijer Supermarkets, Inc., I would be responsible for running grocery, meats, produce, HBC, and the checkout.

With company headquarters close by, I visited the site nearly every day, and after a time I became disheartened to see that not a whole lot of progress was being made in getting the store set up. Although the supermarket kept operating despite the construction, we had to reset and move merchandise more than once during the construction process. Meanwhile, the new store manager couldn't make up his mind and changed things all the time, driving me crazy. A snow fence separated the supermarket from the discount store to keep guests from wandering into the construction area, and as I watched what was happening on the other side, I couldn't keep from offering suggestions. In one incident, I told the store manager where I thought a candy shop should be located, based on my experience in the supermarket. He replied in no uncertain terms, "Mind your own business, food man."

In one sense, he was right. I really did belong on the other side of the snow fence. But more importantly, his response highlighted one of our problems: We were too compartmentalized. It was a classic case of building silos within an organization, and that is a mistake. You have to be able to see all around you and understand where and how you fit into the bigger picture.

> *We were too compartmentalized. It was a classic case of building silos within an organization, and that is a mistake. You have to be able to see all around you and understand where and how you fit into the bigger picture.*

I think by that time, Fred and his father and everyone else began to realize that while the two new executives perhaps had the knowledge to make Thrifty Acres work, they were not doing their jobs successfully.

There was a real cultural difference as well. At the pre-opening meeting, each one got up and introduced himself to the team members as "Mr. So-and-so." Then Fred Meijer stood up, said, "I'm Fred and I want to be called Fred," and went on with his message. Just like that, it became obvious that there was a problem.

IS THERE SOMETHING ELSE
I'M SUPPOSED TO BE DOING?

Coffee breaks at the construction site were held in a small, messy cloakroom. I can remember Mr. Meijer sticking his head in the door one day and finding me drinking a cup of coffee while, a few feet away, the hurricane forces of construction and organization competed and clashed with one another. The next morning, Fred called me into his office. He said, "Dad is a little concerned. Are we okay out there? He felt that you seemed unreasonably calm." What he meant was, "You're just sitting there drinking that cup of coffee, Earl, and we've got problems."

"I don't know what more to do," I told him. "The supermarket's ready. HBC's ready. Checkouts are ready. Is there something else I'm supposed to be doing?"

Earl, 1962

I could see the bells going off in Fred's mind. A day later he called me back in and said, "We'd like you to go and help them get that store ready."

A TOTALLY NEW ANIMAL

Thrifty Acres was a totally new animal in the United States. Everybody else in the business was sure it wouldn't work, but Fred and his dad pressed on nevertheless. Today, we have the sophistication, the financial resources, and the talent to run very complex financial projections before we make a decision. Had we done that back then, however, we probably would not have gone ahead with Thrifty Acres.

I think modern business leaders have to be a combination of risk takers, like Fred and his dad, and careful planners, who study all the possibilities before

49

making a decision. The key to effective leadership is knowing when to take a risk and leap, and when to proceed with caution.

Fred's leadership style recognizes that while he may not be able to sell you

> **The key to effective leadership is knowing when to take a risk and leap and when to proceed with caution.**

completely on his idea, he can persuade you to give it a try. And because he is a risk taker, you want his plan to work. Even if you don't fully believe in it, you will do everything you can to make it work because you believe in Fred.

Our confidence in Fred and ourselves was sorely tested when we didn't do much business on our Thrifty Acres opening day in June 1962. We stood around a nearly empty store. When closing time arrived, around nine or ten o'clock, we hadn't done much business all day. Then came the last straw, an announcement over the public address system: "Ladies and gentlemen, we will be closing in fifteen minutes. Please make your final selections and proceed to the checkout." Whoever I was standing next to, either Fred or his dad, asked, "What did I just hear? We haven't done any business all day and now they're trying to run guests out of the building."

Rushing our guests out was definitely not the Meijer way. Before Meijer was open 24 hours a day, we believed

in opening our doors to guests who arrived before our official opening time and letting guests stay past our closing time. If they were still in the store fifteen minutes after closing, so what? If they were still there thirty mintues later, so what? They were paying guests, and we were in the business of selling them

Grand opening of Thrifty Acres, 1962

merchandise. Our East Coast executives didn't understand this. They had no relationship with our guests, and their bottom-line mentality did nothing to generate guest loyalty.

After Thrifty Acres had been in operation for a few days, it was obvious that we had opened without a clear sense of what we wanted to accomplish or how we would achieve our goal. It was a recipe for disaster, but Fred and Mr. Meijer recognized the problems. Setting out

Thrifty Acres, the first hypermarket in the U.S.A., 1962

to make the necessary changes, Fred concluded that he needed to go back to the people he knew and trusted. He asked Harvey to take care of all sales for the company, and he asked me to be responsible for operations. With that step, Thrifty Acres was on the way to becoming a complete store, not a supermarket and a discount store operated by two separate teams.

I'LL GET IT ALL AT MEIJER

Even as we were ironing out the difficulties facing the original Thrifty Acres, we were building two more stores, both set to open in October 1962. The Muskegon store was housed in a new building, and the Holland store was an enlargement of our existing supermarket. By late 1962, the three Thrifty Acres stores were losing more money than the company's fourteen other supermarkets were earning. Nevertheless, the Meijers were determined to keep going, even refusing an offer for the three stores. They might have been tempted if they had only one Thrifty Acres to walk away from, but they had taken a risk on three stores, and they believed they would ultimately succeed.

We were still a small company at the time, and Fred was always good at communicating, in good times and bad. We all knew we were in trouble, but we just put on our work clothes and worked. We were prepared to do whatever it took. And we eventually turned the whole thing around.

Hendrik and Fred, 1963

First, we faced the reality that the leases negotiated by our East Coast executive were bound to lose us money. A different vendor operated each shop in the discount area, and we weren't getting a sufficient share of the revenue to cover our construction and operating costs. In fact, we couldn't collect enough on their sales to survive. These were leases we couldn't live with, so we decided to run the departments ourselves. First, we bought out the women's apparel lessee and used what little credit we had to buy merchandise. Then, at some point, we began buying shoes and paint. Fred was sure that our team could operate these departments as well as, if not better than, anyone else. And he was right. When we dispensed with licensed operations and took over the ownership and management of these departments, they became profitable.

> *Fred was sure that our team could operate these departments as well as, if not better than, anyone else. And he was right.*

Every day offered a sharp learning curve for all of us. Chuck Westra, who had been a supermarket advertising manager, had to figure out what kind of ads to run. Then there was the matter of the cash registers. The supermarket registers needed only a few basic categories: grocery, meat, produce, tax, and home center. But for Thrifty Acres, we needed a lot of breakdowns to see how each one of the many departments was doing. An early and partial solution was attaching a Kimball ticket to a garment or other piece of merchandise. The ticket was ripped off when the item was sold, and the office would process the tickets, telling us how much of a specific product we sold. The process was only 45 to 50 percent accurate, however, so we turned to a punch-paper tape register, which allowed us to ring up numbers from the Kimball ticket by punching a tape and then reading the punch holes with a special machine.

The cash registers represented one of our earliest moves to technology. And even though our financial resources were tightly limited, company leaders encouraged us to act first and find the money later. Thanks to that can-do attitude, all three stores began making money. By the time we opened our fourth and fifth Thrifty Acres in 1964, this time in Kalamazoo, the business had turned the corner. One store was located on Patterson and Douglas and the other on South

Construction of the first Kalamazoo Thrifty Acres, 1964

Westnedge. At 65,000 or 70,000 square feet, they were small compared with the 235,000 square feet of today's typical Meijer store.

Despite evidence to the contrary, the food industry and some very well-regarded business scholars were convinced that the Thrifty Acres concept would not work. I remember being at a mid-winter Food Marketing Institute (FMI) meeting and introducing myself to a distinguished professor from Harvard who said, "Oh, yes, we were just talking about your stores. I was explaining to these folks that you should be admired for trying, but it isn't going to work because people will not buy groceries and dresses at the same checkout." Had he asked me, I would have agreed that the idea probably wouldn't work. After all, who was I to disagree with a learned Harvard business professor?

I think the concept worked because the market for this unique type of store was there. But, as we discovered, it takes about a year for customer awareness to develop. Now, our guests appreciate the convenience of the

Thrifty Acres, 1965

One-Stop Shopping that Meijer stores provide. Their mindset today is "Why make separate stops at a lot of stores? I need paint, bread and milk, a toy for the birthday party, birthday candles, and a birthday cake. I'll get it all at Meijer. And at a great price."

4

A DECADE OF EXPANSION & EXPERIMENTATION: 1966-1976

GENUINE PLEASURE

When I became vice president of operations in 1966, my goal was to teach store managers what I thought was the right way to run a store, to articulate to them the Meijer way of doing things. That was not difficult. Since I'd gotten to know Fred and his dad, I'd respected the way they did business, and as a store manager, I had learned to enjoy the people side of working at Meijer. Throughout my career, I've had the

Earl, teaching the Meijer way to a group of store managers, c. 1966

chance to provide opportunities to a lot of people. Watching those people grow with the company has been a genuine pleasure.

DON'T TAKE THEIR DIGNITY

I learned a lot from a week-long training program, "Getting Work Done Through People," offered by the Food Marketing Institute, originally known as the Supermarket Institute. It was like a full college term compressed into five days. One of the instructor's principles that I have tried to practice ever since had to do with always treating employees with honesty and dignity, even after you have decided they are not going to be successful with your company. "Don't take away their dignity," he said. "When two of you are on a boat, don't throw the other person overboard. Instead, drop him off in shallow water where he can make it safely to shore."

> *"When two of you are on a boat, don't throw the other person overboard. Instead, drop him off in shallow water where he can make it safely to shore."*

Earl, 1967

I always remembered what he said because it is how I would want to be treated. I tell our people, "Not everyone you hire is going to work out, and when that happens, it's bad enough that you have to tell them, but don't take their dignity, too."

The workshop taught me another important lesson: to value in-service training. I grew immensely that week, and kept the notebook around for years. Since then, I have done my best to see that Meijer team members have access to the training they need to succeed at their jobs.

WE'VE GOT A PROBLEM, FOLKS

Looking back, I realize that sometimes I've felt the most productive and enjoyed myself the most when the Meijer organization confronted its biggest challenges. In those situations, everybody pulls together and has one goal in mind — the company's survival. In 1967, we had one of those challenges.

Meijer had opened two stores in

> *Looking back, I realize that sometimes I've felt the most productive and enjoyed myself the most at times when the Meijer organization confronted its biggest challenges.*

Lansing, and we had made the decision to include large home and garden centers. We hadn't run financial projections to determine the feasibility of our plan, we simply did it, just as the Meijers had throughout the entire history of the company. Fred and his dad believed in expansion, and whenever they could borrow enough money, we'd build another store. So when they wanted to go into home and garden centers, we went ahead.

But we didn't accurately estimate the cost of the added inventory and, as a result, the entire business almost came tumbling down on our heads. We discovered the bad news while attending an FMI meeting in Cleveland. Fred ran into someone from Topco Associates, our buying cooperative, who asked when we were planning to pay our $2 million bill. Fred just blanched. He got on the phone immediately and called our accountant, who confirmed that not only were we short on cash, we were also in serious arrears, to the tune of nearly $3 million. Now, running short of cash was not an emergency — that's the way we lived. But being late paying our bills was a thunderbolt, and we did not have the money to make the payments.

Harvey Lemmen, Fred Meijer, and Earl, 1967

It was serious trouble. We all left the meeting immediately, came home, and started scrounging around for money. Fred called Michigan National Bank to request an immediate loan and learned that Ed Barnes, our banker, was on a fishing trip and could not be reached. The bank said we would get our answer on Saturday morning. So there we sat, Fred Meijer, Harvey Lemmen, and I, in Fred's office at Michigan and Fuller, waiting for the phone to ring. When the call finally came telling us we had been approved for the $2 million loan, three very somber people let out a collective sigh of relief.

I recall thinking at the time that if the bank had said "No," I would be looking for work for the first time in 15 years. Fred, on the other hand, would not only be out of a job, he would lose everything he had.

Since then, I always have thought of Meijer's fortunes as my fortunes, and I try to persuade every Meijer team member to think the same way. I want them to regard each

LEARNING TO LEAD • MY LIFE AND MEIJER

customer as a guest, and each guest as someone who is behind their paychecks. We have to make all guests feel welcome and ensure they

> *I want them to regard each customer as a guest, and each guest as someone who is behind their paychecks.*

want to come back, because while our paychecks come from Meijer, our jobs come from satisfied guests.

Before the crisis ended, Fred shared the news with our team members. To his way of thinking, they were the ones who should know because they were the ones most affected. At our annual awards banquet that year, rather than gloss over what had happened, Fred said, "We have a problem, folks." At every store he visited, he said, "You know, I signed those loan papers 99 times. We borrowed this money, and by golly we have to pay it back." Everyone in the company knew about the problem. More importantly, team members felt they were part of the solution. Fred's openness and honesty caused us to all pull together.

Because of that, we brought our inventories in line and had one of our best years, from the standpoint of profit as a percentage of sales. We closed ranks with one thing in mind — paying off that debt. We were a profitable company, but we had been spending more than we were making. We

> *You don't often see somebody trying to put a puzzle together without using the completed picture as a guide. Fred put the picture in front of the entire company so we could all solve the puzzle together.*

had to get the debt paid off and go on with our expansion. The company's crisis demanded an awful lot of attention and a singleness of purpose from top to bottom. Every team member at every store knew our problem. You don't often see somebody trying to put a puzzle together without using the completed picture as a guide. Fred put the picture in front of the entire company so we could all solve the puzzle together.

60

The lesson learned, according to Fred, was, "We'll never do that again." Ever since then, we have had a clear

Setting the guidelines: Fred Meijer, Earl, Gezina Meier (Fred's mother), and Harvey Lemmen, 1968

set of financial guidelines that set limits on our borrowing. In other words, what we try to do is invest our profit and borrow at a controlled rate. Had those guidelines been in place in 1967, we would not have added the home and garden centers to both Lansing stores at the same time. We would have known we couldn't do it. As a result of that experience, we put those guidelines in place and made them work.

Today we're a very sound company financially. We still borrow money for real estate, and we still follow the same formula. We probably could stretch it some, but if we expanded any faster, we might just get in trouble. However, despite that warning long ago, we also believe you can be too conservative. You can pull your head in to avoid being shelled by competitors' artillery, and you will seem safe. But there's a battle going on that your company may be losing, and you won't even know it.

IT'S YOUR COMPANY, FRED

At some point in the late 1960s, we concluded our stores needed to be open on Sundays. Times were changing, and so much of our competition operated on Sunday that we didn't feel we could afford to stay closed any longer. However, West Michigan is a conservative area, and when we opened our Thrifty Acres stores on Sundays in September 1969, some people became upset.

In retail, it is not enough to understand your business.

You must also understand the communities that form your market. We weren't wrong to open on Sundays from a business perspective, but we had to approach the whole thing cautiously from a community perspective. People wrote letters to complain, and a few churches organized letter-writing campaigns or distributed preprinted cards to be sent to us. We made sure that personal letters got personal responses explaining our position and preprinted cards got a form letter from Meijer.

We also did our best to accommodate team members whose religious convictions made it difficult for them to work on Sundays. It didn't take long to realize we couldn't always predict how team members would respond. I remember preparing to talk with one store manager who was quite religious. I approached the whole thing very cautiously because he was a kind soul and a true believer in his faith. His response taught me you should never anticipate another's behavior.

I said, "If you decide to work, it would be this much overtime for you or whoever's in charge." To my surprise, he quickly agreed to work on Sundays, explaining that the additional income would permit his family to make a larger contribution to their church.

Fred and Lena Meijer, c. 1970

Later, we decided we needed to be open on holidays as well. Once again it was a difficult decision in which we had to balance business considerations with team member, community, and Meijer family concerns. We actually canceled our first holiday opening. It was Thanksgiving and we were geared to open, had ads ready to run, and work schedules set. But Fred's wife, Lena, heard complaints about having to work on the holiday from some of the cashiers. Lena is a sweet, humane person, and she told Fred it bothered her that the cashiers would not be with their families on the holiday. When Fred asked me what to do, I said, "Do you want to stay closed?"

"Can we do that?"

"It's your company, Fred."

So we canceled the opening and changed our plans because the stage was not yet adequately set. We weren't ready to counter the objections, and not everybody agreed with us. The next year, acceptance of the idea had grown. We opened some of the stores on Thanksgiving and other holidays, and the following year we opened the rest of them. Many of our guests welcomed the opportunity to buy a beach cooler on the

> *Our job is to serve the public. It isn't to run the stores at our convenience.*

Fourth of July, for example, or to purchase last-minute items for Thanksgiving dinner. Our job is to serve the public. It isn't to run the stores at our convenience.

VALUABLE LESSONS, EXPENSIVE TUITION

My years as operations director in the 1970s were especially interesting because Meijer was trying many different retail combinations. Thrifty Acres took us from groceries and supermarkets to broader merchandising, but we couldn't decide on the right combination of products and how best to sell them. The result was a variety of stores and expansion schemes that gave me an education in retailing no college curriculum could match. The lessons were not free. Meijer's expenditure of time, effort, and funds was in some cases very costly, but, along with an entire group of Meijer team members, I received knowledge and insight that would serve me well.

Meijer expanded from its Grand Rapids base to other parts of Michigan in the late 1960s and early 1970s. Moving first to the Kalamazoo area in 1964, we entered the

Lansing market in 1967 and extended our reach to the Detroit area in 1974. Each time, we found a niche open to us, but it required work and a significant amount of time before we found our place in the community.

Establishing ourselves outside West Michigan required a greater investment and took far longer than we anticipated. Each time we moved into a new area, we learned more about our stores and how to keep our company growing. Going to Lansing was a major decision because the stores were larger, requiring a greater investment. Similarly, the decision in 1974 to go to Detroit had far-reaching implications. It is a competitive market, and it tested to the limit our will to suceed, as well as our business skills. But we were determined to become a larger company, and expansion into new markets was the most effective strategy for achieving this goal.

In addition to building new Meijer stores, we tried several different types of specialty stores during the decade. Although they were at least marginally successful, we finally concluded that we preferred to operate just one retail concept. We did not, however, reach that

A Meijer Sagebrush store, c. 1976

decision overnight. At one time or another in the 1970s and early 1980s, we operated Sagebrush and Copper Rivet men's clothing stores, Casual Court and Tansy for women's apparel, and Thrifty's Kitchen. We also got into and out of major appliances, men's suits, auto repair shops called TBAs (tires, batteries, and accessories), and Spaar discount drug and general merchandise stores.

Throughout this period, we were looking at possible markets and studying ways to complement the Thrifty Acres stores. We were also seeking the best fit with the values and philosophy that Fred and his dad had always espoused.

When we tried TBAs, for example, we had a hard time finding and keeping mechanics. In an industry largely unregulated at the time, most mechanics wanted to work on a combination salary and commission basis. By convincing people their autos needed major repairs and parts, mechanics could expect a percentage for each "sale" and earn significant income. Although we were willing to pay competitive wages, we did not believe in selling unnecessary parts and service and refused to pay our mechanics a commission. As a result, our stores were often understaffed, with a constantly changing roster of team members.

Similarly, Spaar defined a niche, but it turned out to be a niche we did not feel comfortable filling. We began the venture in 1979 and eventually operated four Spaar stores, two in Grand Rapids and two out of town. Spaar stores were meant to be a convenience for guests that did not live close to a Thrifty Acres.

Even though we were breaking even, the Spaar stores encountered problems right from the beginning. Our warehouses were geared to ship large orders, but to accommodate the Spaar stores, we were shipping a case at a time, and some stores wanted only half a case. In addition, we couldn't decide what the stores should look like and what they should carry.

Finally . . . it became clear to us that we should get back to what we did best — Thrifty Acres and One-Stop Shopping.

All of the senior officers were spending a lot of time on the Spaar stores. Finally, as we had with other ventures, we asked ourselves what success would really mean. Realizing it would take perhaps 20 Spaar stores to equal the revenue of one Thrifty Acres, we acknowledged we were diverting attention and capital from Thrifty Acres. To achieve the kind of scale we wanted would have required hundreds of Spaar stores, and it became clear to us that we should get back to what we did best — Thrifty Acres and One-Stop Shopping.

Although some observers might contend that Meijer
failed at Sagebrush, or Copper Rivet, or Spaar, each one
was a learning experience. Yes, the company paid tuition,
but Fred and his father never objected to the costs. They
always said you have to pay to get an education, and
sometimes we paid dearly. Spaar and the other enterprises
of the 1970s taught us not to fiddle around with small side
businesses. Either go
for the big time or
don't get involved at
all. Getting out of
Spaar and the other
side businesses was
a good decision. We
turned our attention

> *Yes, the company paid tuition, but Fred and his father never objected to the costs. They always said you have to pay to get an education, and sometimes we paid dearly.*

and our funds back to Thrifty Acres, and we concentrated
on building efficient, high-volume stores.

Thanks to a good leadership team, the stores evolved
into better and better machines. Departments were removed
and added, stores were enlarged and layouts were changed,
all to make them better places for our guests, the customers.
What we learned from the Spaar drugstores and all the other
side ventures we applied with great success to our Thrifty
Acres operation.

AS GOOD AS YOUR BOND

In 1961, I began handling labor relations as part of the
operations director's job, and the thread I tried to run
through all of my dealings with unions was a principle
stressed by my father: Your word should be as good as your
bond. Although I soon turned over direct involvement in
labor to Paul Boyer, the principle did not change. For the
past 37 years, I have tried to make sure the unions knew
that we were honest and that, while Fred might not always
agree with our decisions, he would never countermand
them. That kind of backing is critical to our organization.

Integrity is the cornerstone among Meijer executives.
I've heard Fred say that you should not pull the rug from

under the people working for you who make deals —
whether it's real estate, union bargaining, advertising rates,
or the purchase of merchandise. You never embarrass them,
you never make them look bad, and you never reduce or in
any way minimize their ability to represent Meijer.

The Consolidated Independent Union (CIU) Local 951,
formed in 1951, represented Meijer team members for
many years. In 1963, what was then known as the Retail
Clerks International Association (RCIA) decided to run a
campaign at Meijer against the CIU. Our interest was that
our team members had an opportunity to hear all sides of
the issue and then vote for either union. By a margin of six
to one they voted to
stay in the
independent union,
and we continued to
negotiate with the
CIU.

Every few years,
the RCIA would
mount another

The signing of a new contract with the
representatives of Local 951 of the CIU, 1966

campaign, and we tried to make sure that all sides were
heard. Ultimately, in 1978, the RCIA — now called the
United Food and Commercial Workers — gave up trying to
win an election against the CIU and instead got their
supporters to run for office within the independent union.

The strategy worked, and the independent union was
absorbed by the RCIA. Many Meijer team members
objected, and we supported them. A number of court cases
ensued, and we came close to a strike situation because we
weren't sure we would bargain with the new representation.

When the dust settled, we negotiated our first contract
with the international union, keeping in mind all the while
that these union members were first and foremost Meijer
people. Our responsibility was to treat them like Meijer
people, without letting emotions get in the way. For that
reason, I made up my mind to do everything possible to

develop a relationship with the union president. Out of that determination came a tradition of semiannual meetings between labor and management where we could keep the union informed of our future plans and talk about business without talking about problems. I believe that holding such discussions helps avoid the explosion of small issues into major labor-management conflicts, because if union leaders don't understand your thinking, they're not going to understand your position.

I think that unions can better represent our people if they know more of what we are thinking, and I believe those twice-a-year meetings with the union president helped us safely navigate some dangerous waters. That strategy, however, doesn't always work, as the Toledo strike in 1994 demonstrated. That strike was the first one in my career and the first one in the company's history. Although it was a difficult experience, we learned how to operate under those conditions — successfully — but we hope we'll never have to use that knowledge again.

BUILDING A MEIJER TEAM

During the 1970s, the company developed the team that became today's senior leadership. These team members held lower-level positions back then, but were identified as people who could grow professionally and also provide us with essential in-house expertise. Thanks to Meijer's team-oriented culture, we learned confidence in each other and developed an understanding of how to work smoothly together.

Front row (1-r): Jack Koetje, Fritz Kolk, Harold Hans, Fred Welling. Back row (l-r): Earl, Harvey Lemmen, John Balardo, Jim Titesma

One important aspect of the company's growth is the climate of helping each other and sharing equally in

Meijer's success. At the same time, no individual is singled out when things don't go right. The company keeps those individuals who show leadership and gives them room to demonstrate their leadership ability. If they need me to supervise them very closely, then I probably don't need them — I could do the job myself. After Fred challenged me to take a step up early in my career, I have always been able to take on any new responsibility the company gives me.

> *One important aspect of the company's growth is the climate of helping each other and sharing equally in Meijer's success.*

Jack Koetje was the first person I selected to be a district manager when I was moved up to operations director in 1962. Jack had a phenomenal intuitive sense about retail and how to communicate with customers. Retiring several years ago as senior vice president of operations, he was a key part of a lot of growth.

Ray Leach, who was with us for 35 years, started as a produce trainee because we didn't have any other place to put him. He soon became the produce specialist, going from produce department to produce department sharing his expertise. Later, he became a merchandise manager in hard goods. Ultimately, he was in charge of all general merchandise. He made a great contribution to this company, traveling worldwide in his constant pursuit of new resources.

Ray Leach, Earl, and Harold Hans

Harold Hans was part of the team all the way through those rapid growth years. He retired as executive vice president, but still serves us on a consulting basis.

Paul Boyer and Windy Ray both worked in labor relations. Today, Windy runs the entire human resource department. Bob Jager, who is currently senior vice president of operations, came up through the organization and initiated a lot of aggressive new management development programs.

Dave Perron's appointment to Harold Hans' job was a brand new challenge for him. Watching people like Dave develop is fun. Fritz Kolk had been district manager and has been senior vice president of finance and administration for several years. Bob Riley, who began as corporate counsel, today is senior vice president of corporate counsel.

More than 20 years ago, I needed to talk to a member of the Michigan House of Representatives from the Upper Peninsula and instead met with a member of his staff, a young man named Brian Breslin. I was impressed. Subsequently, we hired Brian, who is now senior vice president for government and community affairs. More recently, we were looking for a new leader for our information technology department and were fortunate to find Kevin Holt, who was going to be transferred by his employer but preferred to stay in Grand Rapids. Kevin is now our senior vice president of information technology and services.

Team leadership is a very important concept at Meijer. It is a style of management I learned from my earliest days at the Michigan-Fuller store, when Fred and his dad would call everyone into their office to discuss the latest idea or

> *Team leadership is a very important concept at Meijer. It is a style of management I learned from my earliest days.*

solve a problem. Working together, depending upon each other, and having total confidence in each other is as central to Meijer's success today as it was when Fred and Mr. Meijer were operating a single small store in Greenville, Michigan.

5

LEARNING TO BE PRESIDENT: 1976-1998

IN FIVE YEARS, YOU'LL BE PRESIDENT

My responsibilities hadn't changed a great deal while I was vice president of operations during the early 1970s. There was more of the same, always more, and the front office grew as we expanded, but the type of work I did varied little. I did my best to make distribution and store operations efficient. Harvey Lemmen was general manager and I reported to Harvey.

Harvey Lemmen, Fred Meijer, and Earl, 1975

In 1975, Fred concluded the time was right for Meijer to begin a leadership transition. He called Harvey and me into his office and said, "These are my plans. Harvey, I'd like to make you president, and in five years, Earl, I'd like to make you president."

So for five years I worked with the knowledge that if I didn't screw up too badly, I'd be president of the company. I've always felt that was pretty smart on Fred's part. I was reaching that point where I needed another hurdle, and with his plan, I knew I was going to have plenty of hurdles.

Later, when I decided to retire, I used a similar approach and tried to allow sufficient transition time. It just seems to make good sense to tell people that you appreciate their work, that you want them to stay with your company, and that they are part of your future plans.

> *It just seems to make good sense to tell people that you appreciate their work, that you want them to stay with your company, and that they are part of your future plans.*

In my case, the plan went just as Fred had laid it out. In 1980, I became president.

73

IN TUNE WITH THE TIMES

One of Hendrik Meijer's favorite sayings was, "You must be in tune with the times to succeed." Following that tradition, Meijer increased its guest service by opening our stores 24 hours a day in 1988. Decisions like this are made carefully, and we had been watching the industry both nationally and in our market area. We thought the time was right to make one-stop shopping a 24-hour, 364-day-a-year reality.

For me, the final impetus came while visiting Columbus, Ohio in 1987. As I left our Brice Road store at ten or eleven o'clock one evening, I noticed the Cub store across the street was open 24 hours. Earlier, when we were establishing our business in Columbus, we had enjoyed competition that closed earlier and opened later than we did. We appreciated that. Now the worm had turned. It had been a good day, but as I stood there, my mood fell. "My gosh," I thought, "Here we've got this big investment and we're going to shut it down while Cub keeps doing business all night."

It was suddenly clear to me that a lot happened during the

It was suddenly clear to me that a lot happened during the hours we were closed . . . Life went on around the clock, whether Meijer was open or not.

hours we were closed. People (potential Meijer guests) went to work and came home from work. They stopped somewhere for an early breakfast or a late pizza, or they rented a video. They needed milk or bread, or maybe they just wanted to shop when the store was quiet. Life went on around the clock, whether Meijer was open or not.

Fred and his dad built the business with an aggressive attitude of serving guests whenever they wanted to shop. The move to around-the-clock service was a natural outgrowth of that culture. As soon as I was back in Grand Rapids, Fred and I talked about whether we should consider opening 24 hours. Because we had already given the idea a great deal of thought, we quickly said "Okay."

Just like that, we were into it. But while some of our team members supported the idea, others still needed convincing. Those in sales saw it as a way to increase volume, but Jack Koetje and the district directors saw it as a logistical nightmare.

To reassure the doubters, we took a trip out east to visit a 24-hour operator. Seeing that we were not asking them to invent something brand new, the directors came on board. To make things easier, we waited until after the holiday season before implementing the change. By then everyone was more comfortable with the decision, and Jack did a great job of helping the operations department not only accept the idea, but push it to fruition.

EMBRACING 24-HOUR SERVICE

Opening on Sundays and holidays meant operating just as we did during the week. But now we had to stock while the store was open, and we needed additional personnel in health and beauty care, pharmacy, and every other area of the store. We resolved all those issues and then made modifications over the years. Pharmacy was closed from 10:00 p.m. to 9:00 a.m. Jewelry went unmanned, raising a concern that we would be robbed blind. But I pointed out that some people were doing a pretty good job of that in the daytime already — jewelry has always been a high stock-loss department.

Going to 24-hour service meant adding a night store team leader in each store and a host of co-team leaders for grocery, the bakery/ice cream shop, and the deli/cheese area. We also had to have

One-Stop Shopping, 24 hours a day, seven days a week, 364 days a year

someone on the checkouts and the service desk. I can remember one store director who had been against the idea later arguing with me for more help.

"I've got to keep those checkouts open," he said.

I asked, "Why?"

"Well, because of the guests."

"That's what I thought you said."

Our guests were grateful we were there for them around the clock. We've heard some great stories, including one about an insomniac deciding to do some redecorating in the middle of the night and coming down to Meijer to buy a gallon of paint. Once, when I was in our Indianapolis store and wearing my Meijer badge, a man came up to me in shorts and a golf shirt and said, "I love this store. I stop here at six o'clock in the morning on my way to the golf course."

I was in the Lexington airport recently, talking to the woman running the ticket counter. When she discovered I was from Meijer, she told me of one of her out-of-town cousins on a recent family visit who couldn't sleep and wanted coffee and doughnuts — at three o'clock in the morning. The solution was simple: "Let's go to Meijer."

The process of deciding to open 24 hours a day, 364 days a year certainly confirmed something I strongly believe. When you are making a decision that affects the entire company, you have to give people time to embrace the idea and work through their concerns.

> *When you are making a decision that affects the entire company, you have to give people time to embrace the idea and work through their concerns.*

Even though the wisdom of the change seemed obvious to some of us, others did not see it so clearly. Once they had a little time to get their mind around the idea, they implemented it with far more enthusiasm than if they had merely carried out our decision. Fred and his father worked that way, and it is still the Meijer way.

GROWING OUTSIDE GRAND RAPIDS

Growth has always been an important factor in the Meijer story. Fred never said, "I want to have the biggest company in the United States," but he and his father believed in expanding the company as rapidly as they could. Their philosophy was that it's important for our team members and our competition to know we're healthy and interested in growth. If we don't grow, our most ambitious team members will become stagnant and leave. They want to work at a place where they are allowed to achieve. We have to give people that chance. If you treat them well and find a place for them, they will continue to contribute to the company.

> *If we don't grow, our most ambitious team members will become stagnant and leave. They want to work at a place where they are allowed to achieve. We have to give people that chance.*

One of our primary considerations was how to expand geographically. We talked about slowly expanding outward from Grand Rapids, opening stores throughout Michigan and into neighboring states as we had been doing, or acquiring operations similar to our own. The other possibility was to "leapfrog" to totally new markets in such diverse locations as Orlando, Tampa, and Tulsa. We had a study done and concluded we ought to continue to grow the way we were, rather than try to jump from one geographic area to another.

In the early 1970s, during the OPEC petroleum shortage, Fred had become convinced that gasoline was going to become very expensive, and he rightly worried that our stores were too large and spread too far apart. Out of that concern emerged the idea of a smaller general merchandise store that would stock a limited supply of groceries. We opened the first of these stores, called Meijer Square, in Kalamazoo

Meijer Square store, 1981

and Bay City in 1981, and we were probably the first ones in the market with that type of operation. Both stores were doing moderately well, and it looked like they had a future.

At that point, an investment banker talked to Fred about a company called Twin Fair, which had thirteen or fourteen stores in western Ohio and Kentucky, with a concentration in greater Cincinnati. Twin Fair was based in Buffalo, New York, and also had stores for sale there. I favored the Ohio-Kentucky acquisition but opposed the idea of moving into Buffalo, where the stores were small and situated on inadequate pieces of property. Because Buffalo was so far away, I felt the full acquisition would be more like buying two companies, each of which would gobble up money and management talent.

Twin Fair store, 1981

We were negotiating with the Twin Fair people at the Metro Airport in Detroit when I finally told Fred straight out that I didn't think we should acquire the Buffalo stores. Art Snell, our attorney, favored the entire acquisition. When he overheard me, he challenged my position.

"What's the matter?" he asked. "Aren't you man enough to handle the challenge?"

"No," I said, "I guess I'm not."

Fred asked Harvey if he agreed, which he did, and said, "Then we drop Buffalo." Fortunately, Harvey supported my position.

We acquired the Ohio Twin Fair stores and converted them to Meijer Squares. The process took a lot of time, effort, and money because there was a great deal of inventory to get rid of, and we had to reshelve the merchandise and redo the checkouts and cash registers. The Twin Fair acquisition also included a warehouse that had been an S & H Green Stamp distribution center. The desk

and credenza that Fred still has in his office came from that warehouse. So, the whole deal cost us several million dollars, less the value of those two pieces of furniture. I once told Fred he had the most expensive desk in the company, and the nice thing about it was that he just laughed.

A billboard announcing the grand opening of a Meijer store in Ohio

Going into Ohio has certainly proven to be a good move. At first we expanded some of the stores and lost more money. Finally we started turning things around, and the Meijer Square stores became our base in Ohio.

LET'S GO FOR IT

There was a time in the early 1990s when Fred thought we were missing some opportunities for growth. "Let's go for it," he said. So from 1992 to 1996, we added 39 stores to the 69 we already had. At one point, nearly all those 39 stores were losing money because they were so new. The profit curve was

Meijer in 1996 — 108 stores

turning down and we didn't know where the bottom was going to be. At that point, I said, "Hey, we've got to put the brakes on. We have pushed our boundaries out. Now let's get this absorbed and then we'll go back to normal expansion."

I am really pleased with the way it worked out. We took a hit on the profit and loss statement, but there were only five shareholders to whom I was accountable — the Meijer family — and they put their full faith and support in the program. There were questions, but never doubts. When we cut back and added only four stores in 1997, the profit curve flattened and started coming back up.

I think the most important thing I learned from that experience was that, when you get into rapid growth, you have to be very careful that team members don't suffer as a result.

I think the most important thing I learned from that experience was that when you get into rapid growth, you have to be very careful that team members don't suffer as a result. Sometimes, people fail because they are asked to take jobs that are beyond their skills. Fred has always made it very clear that we take care of these people. When we needed them, they did their best.

I recall an instance when a person we promoted didn't do well and we had to move him back to his old job. It hurt him personally, but we made sure it didn't hurt financially, and we were still able to provide him with an outstanding career position. I believe we have a responsibility to pick a worker who can succeed, and then to work as hard as we can to help that person succeed. That is the supervisor's job.

SEARCHING FOR NEW WAYS

I n the 1990s, some companies tried to grow by gathering a group of unrelated businesses under a single tent. One the best examples of that is Kmart's strategy, which the company has recently abandoned.

Initially, Kmart acquired a whole series of companies including Pace, Builder's Square, Walden Books, Sports Authority, and OfficeMax. All except Pace, which was sold, have since been spun off. Although several of the businesses have become successful as independent companies, they were not successful under a single management. In fact, those companies may have been the stronger part of Kmart.

It is difficult to run a conglomerate of that type. Most companies have moved away from the concept because it places a great demand on talent and capital resources. That's why I don't think diversification is the answer for our future. Meijer should grow by extending the kind of businesses we are in. Since we are a distributor of consumable and non-consumable goods to the public, and it is not likely that the consumption will cease, we should be searching for new ways to distribute those goods.

A CONVENIENT SOLUTION

I read someplace of a marketing professor who said that supercenters are not convenient places to shop. I think his comments were made in ignorance because large Meijer stores are the most convenient places to shop. At one Meijer store, a guest can buy bread and milk, fill a prescription, treat a loved one to fresh flowers, stock the medicine cabinet with toothpaste and other necessities, and bring home a garden tool. All of these goods are available at one place, relieving

Meijer, 1992

shoppers of the need to make separate stops at various locations, and eliminating the long walk that accompanies a visit to a mall. So when it comes to convenience, there is no more convenient shopping place than a Meijer store.

I really recognized that when visiting my daughter in Chattanooga, Tennessee. I spent all day running from store to store getting supplies. At home, I would have gone to one store and found everything I needed. When I got back to her house, I thought, "Gee, they need a Meijer store here."

MANAGEMENT IS AS IMPORTANT AS TECHNOLOGY

Ever since my early days in operations, I've felt efficient distribution was an important key to retail success. By 1974, our Grand Rapids distribution center (warehouse and inventory control) in Walker, on the city's northwest side, had grown to about

Meijer corporate offices and distribution center in Walker, 1978

500,000 square feet, and we needed more space. We also needed a better location, closer to most of our stores and our areas of growth. By then, Lansing was the geographic center of our company, so that is where we decided to build a second warehouse.

The Lansing grocery warehouse is an interesting building. For instance, it has prefabricated tilt-up walls, which were not very common at the time it was built. The construction team poured the concrete floor first, laid the forms for the wall panels on the floor, poured them, and tilted them up into place. They created panels for the exterior of the building by placing a layer of stone on sand, pouring that form full of concrete, and, when it was cured, tilting the panel up to form the wall. Today,

Construction of the Lansing grocery warehouse

all our stores are built with tilt-up walls, although they are manufactured elsewhere and trucked in.

The Ordermatic system

The warehouse superintendent and I had done a lot of research, and the big thing in warehousing at the time was mechanization. We studied a number of systems and ended up buying one out of Pennsylvania called SI Ordermatic. It was run by computer and functioned like a massive, inverted vending machine. About two football fields long, it was a series of roller conveyors leading to other conveyors that led to loading stations. For example, when two cases of size 303 Food Club Cream Style Corn were called for, the gate would open and let two cases slip out onto the conveyor track and begin their way to the loading dock.

The Ordermatic system was an entirely new concept in warehousing at the time. Only two Ordermatic systems were in operation nationwide when we constructed the Lansing warehouse, and both were experiencing significant problems. We believed our detailed planning would avoid the problems at these other installations, so we went ahead with our plans.

I felt extremely nervous about the Ordermatic system — understandably, because the company had bought it on my recommendation. I remember Harvey Lemmen laughingly asking what I would do if it failed. I laughed in response and said, "If it doesn't work you can get rid of me, but you still won't get the groceries out to the stores." That's when everyone realized how crucial that machine was to our entire operation.

There were some anxious moments, but overall the Ordermatic was a great launch. One of the things I learned

> *One of the things I learned from it was that management is at least as important as technology, and perhaps more important.*

from it was that management is at least as important as technology, and perhaps more important. Ordermatic was a very high-tech machine and took a different kind of management. Fortunately, we had the right people for the job.

We made Ordermatic work because of Paul Boyer, who was moved from labor relations to distribution. Like me, he didn't know how to spell warehouse when he started, but he learned quickly and provided the discipline to run it. In fact, running a warehouse with the Ordermatic required better management than a conventional labor-intensive warehouse did. It took mental discipline and strict maintenance routines to stay on top of its complex computer systems and scheduling logistics, and Paul made it work. Eventually, we replaced the Ordermatic with high-cube storage, which is labor intensive but more efficient. Although we switched to less mechanization and more people in our distribution facilities, we still place the same emphasis on distribution and its management.

SCANNING FOR SUCCESS

Check lane scanners, another technological marvel, had been an immediate success when we introduced them at our original Thrifty Acres store in 1977. Before long, we were using that same technology to get the right product to the right place at the right time, while remaining competitive by lowering the cost of goods.

Managed Replenishment Systems (MRS) was introduced in 1989 in order to get goods from the supplier to the store with as few stops and as quickly as possible. Take the example of a Huffy bicycle. The purchase and replenishment cycle begins when a guest takes the bicycle to the checkout. The bar code ticket is scanned, and the scanner recognizes the universal product code (UPC) as a Huffy bicycle. Using the daily information about sales from Huffy bicycles, new orders are written and transmitted via Electronic Data Interchange (EDI) directly to the vendor.

Huffy then ships the bicycles to the Meijer Retail Support Center, where they are loaded into trucks going to restock Meijer stores.

A Meijer truck, 1998

When we first installed it, we were able to use this quick response system to order 20,000 items and communicate with more than 1,000 vendors through EDI. The numbers doubled within a year and continued to grow. Those were leading breakthroughs for our industry and helped us stay competitive as other costs continued to rise.

Another type of quick response is "drop ship," which enables our suppliers to deliver the product right to our store. Once again, the process begins with guest demand. Each time a product is sold, the check lane scanner reads information from the bar-coded UPC and a replacement is ordered. About 8,000 products were ordered in that way in 1990, and the number has grown ever since.

We have also used Computer Assisted Ordering (CAO) for several years. Again, checkout scanners read the UPC. Orders are transmitted to the Meijer distribution center, where goods are selected, shipped, and restocked within 24 hours. Because CAO merchandise spends time in a warehouse and doesn't use EDI, we don't regard it as part of our quick-response system.

Now, the sale price is programmed into the cash register scanning system, and we use in-store signs to inform guests of the sale price . . . We end up with better records and labor savings.

Scanners have also made changing prices more efficient. Each week we advertise about

1,000 reduced-price sale items. Until recently, we had to record and re-mark every one of those items to the sale price and then mark them again after the sale, a process that used 250 hours each week in each store. Now, the sale price is programmed into the cash register scanning system, and we use in-store signs to inform guests of the sale price. When the item is scanned, the sale price is charged and accounting records are maintained via computer. The process takes only ten hours each week in each store. We end up with better records and labor savings.

EXPANDING DISTRIBUTION

Today, I think we have the most efficient logistical system in the United States. We've always invested the funds necessary to assure the best distribution system. Recently, Paul Boyer took me to Minnesota to look at an operation for cross docking that runs entirely with conveyors. Instead of bringing a product in, storing it, and shipping it when somebody in the stores wants it, this system is based on pre-orders. You bring in the goods, spread them across the dock, and send them right back out on trucks to the stores. You might have a truck sitting at the dock with 1,500 cases of product that are going to go to 30 stores. Instead of being warehoused, the merchandise shoots down tracks and is automatically diverted to areas designated for specific stores. You can have 20 trucks from different suppliers coming in and loading onto that conveyor, with all the merchandise getting meshed together and shooting out to the trucks that will deliver it to the stores. Where we used to have 25,000 square feet of paper diapers in distribution facilities, we don't have any today. So, our need for warehousing space has been greatly reduced.

We base orders on our best projections, and our aim

Meijer Retail Support Center

is that when a product comes in, it immediately goes back out. But if, for example, store sales at Greenville have dropped a little bit on a Procter and Gamble product and store sales at Traverse City have increased for that product by the time the truck arrives, we can adjust the distribution by having the computer look again at the store's post-order distribution needs. Post-order distribution is a great system, but a lot of companies can't do it because they don't have enough volume per store, or they lack the discipline to do it. At Meijer, the system has proven to be a behind-the-scenes success.

MAKE IT READY TO GO

I n addition to the scanner-based ordering and distribution system, we also installed a source-marking system so that merchandise comes to the stores ready to go on the floor. For example, instead of sending garments to the store and unpacking them, tagging them, and putting them on a rack, we centralized the work. In other words, instead of sending three dresses of each size to each store, we'll bring in 150 dresses, unpack, tag and hang them on special garment

> *More than once, we've pushed on despite the comments of critics and naysayers, and we've succeeded because we didn't know any better.*

racks ready for shipping to each store, where they are immediately put on the sales floor. We were told it couldn't be done, that the system wouldn't work, but we've succeeded. More than once, we've pushed on despite the comments of critics and naysayers, and we've succeeded because we didn't know any better.

SOURCECLUB:
LEARNING FROM A NEGATIVE EXPERIENCE

S ourceClub proved we can learn from a negative experience. At one time, I thought warehouse clubs would be the next step in the evolution of discount retailing. If you go back in retail history to the 1950s, department stores carried vast selections, while discounters, or mass merchants, carried very narrow selections. Department stores were large, lovely stores. At the JL Hudson store in Detroit, a doorman greeted customers and elevator operators wore white gloves. The store offered free delivery throughout the Detroit area and created phenomenal Christmas displays in its windows. The discounters had none of that. In those days, too often they simply bought cheap product and sold it cheap. Over time, self-serve department stores such as Meijer and Target evolved into businesses that offer quality merchandise at a true value.

The discounters have become what I regard as the self-service department store. Taking over a great part of the department store's business, they don't carry as wide a range of products as conventional department stores, but they do a very good job of carrying product and keeping their cost of doing business down.

The self-serve department store flourished for quite a few years. Then a company on the West Coast called Price Club, started by a man named Sol Price, opened a warehouse store where you bought a membership that gave you the right to go into the building and buy products at discount prices. Sol Price did a good job of it, and Price Club became a sizable company. Soon, another warehouse club called Costco also started on the West Coast. These ventures were followed by others on the East Coast, and then Wal-Mart started its version, Sam's Club, and Kmart started Pace.

Along with others, I was concerned that this new wave would take a lot of business away from self-serve department stores and our supercenter stores, just as self-serve department stores took it away from conventional department

A groundbreaking ceremony for SourceClub

Meijer SourceClub

stores. There were some who believed the self-serve department store had reached its apex and was on the other side of the bell curve and on the way down. I was worried that five or ten years down the road, wholesale clubs would be prospering while discount stores attempted to figure out what had happened to their niche. Because of this belief, I lobbied for us to enter the warehouse club business.

Once we made the decision, we went full bore. At first we tried to buy Wholesale Club, a company headquartered in Indianapolis, Indiana, but Sam's Club bought that out from under us. From there we started up a division called SourceClub. The people who were working on that put their heart and soul into it. But to be honest, our initiative was too little, too late with an idea that turned out to have wide but shallow appeal. Although wholesale clubs are still present, you don't see multiple warehouse clubs surviving in many markets. Actually, there has been quite a shakeout. Wal-Mart bought Pace from Kmart. Price Club and Costco merged, with Costco the surviving company. So now, Costco and Sam's Club share the niche, and Sam's has struggled for the last few years.

Probably because of my prodding, we made a bad decision to go into SourceClub. I want my fair share of credit, then, that we also made a quick decision to get out. So, the first decision cost a lot of money and the second decision saved a lot of money. And the curve of warehouse clubs passed. We failed in that effort, but we did our best to

> *So, the first decision cost a lot of money and the second decision saved a lot of money . . . but we did our best to see that no one with the company got hurt.*

see that no one with the company got hurt. Paul Boyer was president of SourceClub, and is now doing an outstanding job as executive vice president with our company.

I've rarely heard more compliments about something our organization did than when we decided to get out of SourceClub. Although the dollar loss was substantial, the larger loss would have been if it had caused a reaction that prevented people from promoting

For me, it was reinforcement of the notion that an organization has to find a balance between encouraging reckless risk taking and making people feel very comfortable with intelligent risks.

new ideas. That would be a much, much greater loss than what we lost on SourceClub, and I don't believe that happened. Nobody associated with SourceClub got lined up against a wall, no messengers were shot, none of the executives were chastised. We just admitted it didn't work, and moved on. For me, it was reinforcement of the notion that an organization has to find a balance between encouraging reckless risk taking and making people feel very comfortable with intelligent risks. Otherwise they'll miss the next big idea.

E-COMMERCE

Lately, I've been thinking that the next big idea may be a foray into electronic commerce. It has to happen. Two or three years ago, I encouraged our folks to experiment with e-commerce, knowing it wasn't going to be profitable, but that it would be a learning experience. Unfortunately, our heart and soul was not in it, and it didn't work.

That may have been a little early for e-commerce. There's a learning curve still going on, and what you keep hearing is that everyone's getting into it and there's a lot of speculation, but no one's making a lot of money yet.

I recently read about Barnes & Noble's aggressive entry into the electronic book business. Except, if you call that success, you have to remember many electronic companies are still losing millions of dollars a year. They are very speculative companies whose founders make money because investors choose to speculate in their future.

E-commerce has great potential. Although it will not replace the volume of our stores, it may potentially represent a large part of our business. However, I don't think the food side of e-commerce is going to be nearly as large as some consultants would have us believe.

JUST ONE WORD: PLASTIC

Back in the 1970s, there was a famous movie scene that included the line, "I have just one word for you, young man: plastic." We think that was good advice. It was our determination to stay in tune with the times that led to the development of the Meijer One card. The magnetic strip on the back of the card contains all the necessary information about the guest and

provides guests access to a variety of store services using a four-digit Personal Identification Number (PIN). For instance, guests can use the Meijer One card as an electronic checking (debit) card that transfers funds directly to Meijer. Since we handle over a billion checks a year, and each paper check is handled four times, the savings in time and money is tremendous. I think Hendrik Meijer would agree our use of plastic is one means of "staying in tune with the times."

> *It was our determination to stay in tune with the times that led to the development of the Meijer One card . . . I think Hendrik Meijer would agree . . .*

On the same note, we will also be offering gift certificates on plastic smart cards instead of traditional paper certificates. Scheduled to be implemented in 1999, smart cards provide benefits for both Meijer and our guests. On our end, electronic smart cards are easier and quicker to handle. For guests, it becomes much easier to make incremental purcases. Say a guest with a $50 smart card wants to buy only $10 worth of goods. The card is swiped through the electronic payment system and the $10 is automatically deducted from the value of the card, leaving the guest with a $40 credit still available on the card. I think it will be a winner.

WE HAVE TO KEEP CHANGING THE BOX

We also have to be very alert and willing to take risks when it comes to redesigning our stores. We have to keep changing the box, inside and out. From our first stores in small communities to Thrifty Acres and on to our current store design and retail configuration, Meijer has gone through remarkable changes. Store design has been critical to our success, and we must continue to be very flexible in changing and constantly evolving what we know as a Meijer store. Our latest effort, Design 2000, represents exciting innovations, both inside and out. Just as with earlier efforts, some of those ideas are going to work, and some of them won't.

Our next store will have some of those ideas. As an example, for a long time we've been very rigid about where the pharmacy was located because we wanted it near health and beauty care, which we've always felt needed to be next to groceries. Now, the pharmacy and health and beauty care will be in the front of the store, but on the opposite side from groceries. So, everybody who

Earl, 1996

used to complain that the pharmacy was inconvenient because it was in the back of the store will be happy because it's in the front of the store, and everybody who's used to having it as part of their grocery-shopping trip will complain because it's on the other side of the store.

Design 2000 is most certainly not the last word. We will continue to work on store design, just as we will continue to seek increasingly efficient distribution systems and new marketing ideas. But regardless

Design 2000 — the store of the future

of how hard we try, we will never find a way to please every guest by putting all our merchandise next to the front door.

6

REFLECTIONS
& VISION

THREE GENERATIONS OF LEARNING

I will always treasure my 46-year association with Meijer. It has given me the unique and delightful experience of working with three generations of the Meijer family. Hendrik Meijer was a unique individual who pioneered a new way of grocery retailing. I recall fondly the times he talked with me and explained his business philosophy. In his turn, Fred Meijer totally redefined the company. As my mentor, Fred showed phenomenal patience while teaching and guiding me to my maximum potential.

Although my bonds with Fred's sons, Doug, Hank, and Mark, may not be as close, my relationship with each generation is special and meaningful. They are nice people who care about others

Earl and Fred Meijer, 1996

and truly want to help people succeed in life. As I see it, my goal, and that of my successors, should be to enhance and perpetuate the corporate culture the Meijer family has created.

COURTESY IS CONTAGIOUS

The Meijer culture respects individual dignity, encourages initiative, recognizes integrity, forgives human frailty, and rewards dedicated service. Courtesy and fair treatment are contagious. The key to the Meijer culture lies in understanding that when a team member is treated well and fairly, that team member will treat fellow team members and Meijer guests the same way. I learned that principle early in my career at Meijer when I was not fired for mistakes in my first position, and through the promotions and rewards I received over the next 46 years. Chances are, if your boss treats you well, even when you make mistakes, then you will treat others similarly.

Each of us at all levels in the company must understand that it is essential to treat people who report to us just as we wish to be treated by our supervisors. I have a grandson who has just started working for Meijer as a bagger, and I love to hear him talk about the fun things he's learning in his job. He's an important part of the Meijer image, the last position in the guest-service line, so how he feels about his job, his supervisor, and his fellow team members plays a big part in how he treats Meijer guests.

Earl's grandson, Russty Holton

One of the biggest challenges facing Meijer management is demonstrating to each team member the impact he or she has on the entire organization. Every interaction between a team member and a guest is an opportunity to make a favorable impression, which in turn builds loyalty.

PLEASE, TELL ME EVERYTHING

I know how easy it is to view guests as a mass of people. This perspective hurts the company, though, because when we view guests this way, soon we begin treating them like a mass of people as well. But guests aren't a mass. They're individuals who happen to be brought together under a single roof — ours. Each one has made a choice to shop at our store. We need to act the part of a gracious host and make each one feel welcome.

Ultimately, management must clarify for each employee our dependency on our guests. They certainly can get along without Meijer, but Meijer would soon fold without our guests. Thinking of guests as the source of our paychecks reminds team

Thinking of guests as the source of our paychecks reminds team members to treat each one with the respect, friendliness, and helpfulness they deserve.

98

members to treat each one with the respect, friendliness, and helpfulness they deserve.

In many ways, guests know us better than we know ourselves. They also possess the objectivity to tell us what we're doing right and what we're doing wrong. Whenever a guest is generous enough to provide this kind of input, we should always pay attention.

I recently had the chance to do just that. Flying back to Grand Rapids from somewhere, I sat next to a woman who lives in Grand Haven. When I told her I worked at Meijer, she mentioned a couple of problems she had with one of our stores. Then she said, "You know, I shouldn't have done that. I've just met you, and here I am complaining."

I replied, "I want to hear everything you have to say. You're in the store regularly and see it from a guest's point of view, so you're in the best position to tell me how we can do better. So, please, go ahead and tell me everything."

MEIJER PEOPLE

W hen I look at the Meijer work force, I see a solid group of great people. Every one of them has a unique personality and special interests. I have always enjoyed getting to know individual team members or learning about them from their supervisors. The individuals who work at Meijer reflect the diversity and goodwill that is our greatest single asset.

Earl with a Meijer team member

One of them, Dennis Bumstead, has been on my mind these days. Dennis was hearing- and vision-challenged, but somebody had the good sense to hire him to work in the warehouse, where he was a very good team member for about 25 years. By a cruel twist of fate, his life was cut short. Dennis frequented a little bar on Grand Rapids' west side, where a woman who knew sign language befriended him. One night, as he left the bar, he discovered a couple of guys beating up his friend. He tried to stop them, and as a result was beaten and died of the injuries. Although I never met him, I have no doubt he was a great person. He was a Meijer person, living a good life, doing the right things. This company is full of people like that.

I had a wonderful experience during a recent visit to one of our Indianapolis stores. I was talking with the store director when somebody brought a greeter over for me to meet. This fellow had spent nearly 40 years working in a steel mill, but he was absolutely right for his new job as a greeter. He works hard to ensure that guests receive good service. We had lunch together, and his enthusiasm made my day. "I wish I was 40 years

A Meijer greeter

younger," he said, "and that I could have gone to work with Meijer back then." I enjoy meeting team members like that.

Indianapolis store director Rob Jager is a second-generation Meijer team member. His father, Bob Jager, is senior vice president of operations. Before Rob was promoted to store director, I asked his father, "How come your son doesn't have his own store? Everybody speaks well of him and he seems to be doing a good job. Are you holding him back because you're trying to avoid any complaint about nepotism?"

"Well, yes."

"Quite frankly," I told him, "Meijer is losing on that one. I think he ought to be a store director." Getting the go-ahead to promote his son was a real relief to Bob. Rob was young and somewhat inexperienced, but he's doing a fine job. He has a quality we seek in every Meijer team member: people like him.

WALKING AROUND

When I was a district manager, I told my store managers to tour their stores first thing every day, greeting every person and checking conditions. Of course, Meijer operated supermarkets then, not 240,000-square-foot combination grocery and general merchandise stores. Today, there are many more things to cover on a store tour, but I still like to see the night manager and the day manager touring the store together as they make the transition from one shift to another.

I love retailing. In fact, I really missed the stores when I went to the office. Sales drive our business, and if you don't have the right people, you don't get the sales. If you don't have the right people, you don't get the profits. If you don't have the right people, you don't build the right kind of stores. If you don't have the right people, the stores aren't managed right. I want to feel right when I walk around a store, and when I do, it's because of the people. The feeling starts in the parking lot. If things are messy around the front door, your guests will not have a good attitude when they get inside the door. If team members are not alert to what's going on everywhere on the premises, the store isn't being well managed.

KNOW WHAT'S GOING ON

Because of my background, I believed that store visits were one of the top priorities of my job. You can't make good decisions for the company if you don't know firsthand what is going on in the stores. Meijer has always placed a great deal of importance on all levels of management making frequent store visits. Mr. Meijer and Fred did it

You can't make good decisions for the company if you don't know firsthand what is going on in the stores.

all the time, and I picked up the habit from them. It's so much a part of me that I'm sure I'll continue doing it automatically after I retire.

When I was a store manager, some of my fellow managers would sound an alert to their crews if they got word that Mr. Meijer, Fred, or a supervisor was in the area. Some even had a special paging code to alert them to the visit. I didn't believe in doing that. I was not going to run the store differently just because there was a supervisor around. If our stores are run to make guests happy, that should make supervisors happy.

As Meijer president, I tried to spend a third of my time in the stores. Whenever I was on the road and there was a store nearby, I stopped in for a visit. I tried to keep my schedule open on Fridays for visiting stores. As part of my holiday time, I would hit the road and go to the outlying stores. Meijer family members also visit stores. I think it's important that team members in each store see that management supports them. They are important to Meijer's success, and they deserve to see somebody from the office.

> *I think it's important that team members in each store see that management supports them. They are important to Meijer's success . . .*

One year, I took a three-day Thanksgiving trip to Ohio by car. I pulled into our Lima, Ohio, store at 11:30 p.m., and there stood the store director with her coat on her arm, talking to the night manager, handing the store over to him for the night. I felt good letting them know we appreciated their attentiveness. I was able to hit that store again at six o'clock the next morning while the night crew was still there. Frankly, they were very surprised to see the company president, but I think they appreciated my presence. I know we appreciate theirs.

It is important to visit all stores, not just the most convenient, or the newest ones. A friend once said to me,

"You know, when I go into your new store in Grand Rapids, I always see suits, but when I go into an older store, I never see suits." What she meant by "suits" was people from the front office.

"Oops," I thought. If she noticed the absence of suits at one store, we have a problem. So I checked my visiting schedule, where I keep a record of every store visit. Sure enough, I didn't have enough check marks in that older store's slot. Subconsciously, visiting the older store wasn't as much fun. We watch that more closely now.

FEELING COMFORTABLE ABOUT CHANGE

Leadership transition is a critical juncture in any company's life. Prior to my retirement, Meijer had gone through two very smooth, almost seamless transitions: one when Mr. Meijer stepped aside without fanfare to let Fred take over the company, and the other when Fred informed Harvey and me how succession would evolve when he decided to hand over the reins of day-to-day company management. When I decided to step down as president, I was determined to continue that tradition.

Fred has said a number of times he doesn't know when his dad put him in charge. I don't know when he did either, but I know when I came to the company Fred was taking charge. There was no formal announcement, it just happened. Just as Hendrik Meijer was no less an influence for having turned over daily operations to his son, so when Fred left things in Harvey's hands, he did not diminish his own stature. Similarly, Harvey Lemmen's opinions are still highly regarded at Meijer.

I learned it was possible to transfer leadership without disruption, and I tried to pattern my own transition after their example.

From observing how Mr. Meijer and Fred handled the situation, I learned it was possible to transfer leadership without disruption, and I tried to pattern my own transition after their example.

I can't say exactly what triggered my decision to retire, but shortly after my sixtieth birthday, after a lot of discussion with Donnalee, I sat down with the Meijer family and told them that I would retire when I was sixty-five. Although I felt good about my job performance, I also knew that I didn't feel quite as sharp as I had when I was fifty. I had felt really strong at fifty, with a lot of experience and a reasonable amount of knowledge and confidence. At sixty I still felt strong, but I suspected that in another five years it would be time to turn my duties over to younger minds and leaders.

Earl and Donnalee, 1997

I believed I owed it to the company and the family to let them know when I would be leaving so that we could proceed with whatever needed to be done to assure an orderly succession. Once I made that commitment, I also promised myself that I wouldn't change it. I wouldn't extend the deadline, I wouldn't ask to stay "for a little while longer."

SIDE-BY-SIDE

From the first moment, Meijer looked to its own ranks for my replacement. Everyone agreed on the importance of avoiding a person who comes in from the outside, knows nothing about the company's history and operation, and may be tempted to build a brand new leadership team. We wanted someone who would help to perpetuate the Meijer culture. We wanted a "people" person, and we identified several internal candidates who filled the bill.

A little less than a year before I retired, Jim McLean was selected as my successor. It's unusual for an organization to have the two top people working side-by-side for that length of time, but it's a practiced pattern at Meijer. Once that decision had been made, my primary task was to make sure senior officers were comfortable

Jim McLean and Earl, 1998

and to reassure them that the team would remain intact except for one member — me. I knew the team had concerns that my replacement would think and act differently, and I wanted them to see I was comfortable with the change. I also wanted them to feel comfortable about changing the company without worrying how I would feel. Meijer team members now have a new leader.

In 1998, the senior executive team spent two days together discussing the future of the company. I told them, "There isn't anybody else around to decide where this company is going. You're it. You will have major input from owners, but as senior officers, you will gather information from all available sources and then decide the company's future direction."

Jim has great human instincts, *excellent* human instincts. That was something we looked for in a successor. We wanted somebody a little more outgoing than I am, somebody eager to perpetuate the Meijer culture, and smart enough to hire the necessary expertise. I always felt that what I didn't know, I could hire, as long as I was smart enough to realize I didn't know it.

> *I always felt that what I didn't know, I could hire, as long as I was smart enough to realize I didn't know it.*

Of course, that can be a problem. If your ego is so big that you can't admit when you don't know something, then it will get in the way. That's not a problem for Jim, who has the intellect to know when he needs to hire other people who can do things better than he can.

COMMUNITY OBLIGATIONS

While the primary obligation of any business is to earn a profit for shareholders, it also has a responsibility to support the cultural and social organizations in its community. Meijer gladly fulfills this responsibility both with financial contributions — Meijer is a generous business citizen — and through volunteering and leadership service by its team members.

Meijer believes in and supports the strong community culture in Grand Rapids, the city where the company is headquartered. We join a long list of other

*The Frederik Meijer Building,
Meijer Corporate Headquarters*

public and private companies in the area with impressive records of involvement at the local level. For all of these companies, particularly the privately owned ones, Grand Rapids is where we live as well as work, which closely links corporate and community decision making.

Grand Rapids also offers a diversity lacking in many cities. I've traveled to dozens of cities that rely on a single large corporation, a university, or a state capitol to provide economic and cultural activity. With a broad base of locally owned companies across a spectrum of industries, Grand Rapids enjoys stability, growth, and opportunity from numerous sources, which in turn makes the area attractive to the best professional talent. The more I travel, the more I'm convinced that Grand Rapids is the ideal location for

Meijer headquarters.

Meijer encourages all its family members, senior officers, and team members to be active community members. In our family, Donnalee has been an active community volunteer for many years and was honored in 1998 at a community-wide salute by the Grand Rapids YWCA. I was less active earlier in my career, but once I became president, my position called for me to participate in numerous community activities. As a result, I have broadened my view of community service and its place in a corporate culture. Through my community service, I have also come to believe that volunteerism makes for a more well-rounded individual and produces a better community in which to live and do business.

I've been very careful in taking on outside activities. Capital campaigns, for example, are something I'm not very comfortable with because I have trouble asking for

Grand Rapids Public Museum

money. I think it's because my dad was always asking for money in the church. Despite my general reluctance, I've been privileged to be involved in three such campaigns, one on behalf of the Public Museum of Grand Rapids and two at the Frederik Meijer Gardens. The museum was my first

Three Clowns and the Lena Meijer Conservatory at the Frederik Meijer Gardens

experience with a capital campaign, and I have to say I was gratified when we opened that splendid new facility. The gardens are really special to Fred, so I wanted to participate in those campaigns for that reason.

THE FUTURE IS CONTINUALLY IMPROVING

Although I have turned the Meijer presidency over to Jim McLean, and this small book is about history and my 46 years with Meijer, my thoughts remain focused as much on the future as they are on the past. I have seen incredible changes in food and general merchandise retailing since the time I was hired as a clerk at Meijer's Cedar Springs store in 1952. At that time, there were only 214 team members in the entire company, which consisted of six supermarkets. Food products seldom came in more than two sizes, cash registers had only three or four department keys, government regulations were minimal, and customers paid in cash. Today there are 118 Meijer stores, more than 79,000 team members, computerized cash registers constantly monitor inventories, and stores don't simply sell products, they merchandise a complex "attribute mix" of various components for different market segments.

I believe the future will also see Meijer working continually to improve its ability to provide a full assortment of quality merchandise at the best possible price, in the most convenient setting.

I see Meijer continuing for some time as a very successful, progressive mass merchant, or self-serve store, with a lot of refining continuing on a regular basis. For that reason, I expect to see many new generations of store design. I think that's one of our healthy points, even though it's expensive. I believe the future will also see Meijer working continually to improve its ability to provide a full assortment of quality merchandise at the best possible price, in the most convenient setting.

THE ARGUMENT OF CONVENIENCE

A professor recently wrote an article arguing that big stores eventually will fail. Their large size, he claims, overwhelms consumers, who see them as inconvenient. Given a choice, they'd rather shop at smaller stores than larger ones.

A Meijer store, 1997

I've thought about this article for awhile, and I'll admit that I just don't follow the professor's logic. In my opinion, getting in my car and driving to a second, third, and fourth retailer is far more inconvenient than crossing a 240,000-square-foot store. Plus, I only have to wait in one checkout line, and I only have to load my purchases into my car once.

The article makes some sense when applied to the guest who is buying just one or two items, but even then, I think Meijer is just as convenient as a typical suburban grocery store. A guest who knows which side of our store to park on and can be in and out very quickly, perhaps even more quickly than a competing specialty store because we'll have more checkout lanes open. Granted, we're not going to be as fast as a corner convenience store for that kind of shopping trip, but in most cases, One-Stop Shopping offers guests a convenience advantage, and I think this is a big reason why Meijer has done so well.

I have another, more compelling reason why the professor is wrong. Several retailers, including a couple of well-known international discount chains, have begun building stores very similar to a Meijer store, with general merchandise and a full grocery under a single roof. I doubt they would go to the trouble and expense unless they had researched the idea thoroughly and found that it offers compelling profit potential. I suspect the retail professionals at these companies have a much better grasp of the marketplace than the professor. They had better, because huge sums of investment capital are at stake.

I take this new competition more seriously than I do the possibility that our guests will someday abandon us for smaller stores. Throughout Meijer's history, the company has always found ways to differentiate itself from the competition. It looks like the biggest tests of this ability are yet to come.

AHEAD OF THE COMPETITION

I can guarantee you that senior management keeps a close eye on the competition and works tirelessly to keep Meijer one step ahead. We know that the minute the company stops innovating, even momentarily, our competitive advantage will disappear. Someone will catch us.

> *The minute the company stops innovating, even momentarily, our competitive advantage will disappear. Someone will catch us.*

Competition poses a very serious threat, but our team members are equal to the task. You can see this for yourself just by watching what happens at the Meijer stores in your area. Every change, every improvement, is designed specifically to enhance your shopping experiences. And since change is constant these days, let me encourage you to shop frequently at Meijer so you can stay on top of all the changes taking place.

Our competitive capabilities are particularly put to the test when we enter a new market. We're starting from scratch, while our competitors have the advantage of familiarity. We need to make sure new stores combine an entertainment factor, a value factor, and a convenience factor into a package tempting enough to lure guests through our doors.

The West Chester, Ohio, Meijer store, c. 1996

Even then, our job is only half-done. Once they visit us, we need to impress them enough that they return a second time, then a third, and so on. A big advertising campaign can draw guests, but only a competitively superior store can build the guest

> *Probably the biggest challenge facing every team member today is performing his or her job in a way that contributes to the company's competitive advantages.*

loyalty that is vital to its long-term success. Probably the biggest challenge facing every team member today is performing his or her job in a way that contributes to the company's competitive advantages. It's something we all need to think about constantly.

Competition is very serious. Often, it's fun, too. I particularly enjoy planning and implementing new services for our guests, such as the Meijer One card, credit card payment options, store redesigns, and so on. As Meijer makes changes that will secure its future, the company will continue to adopt innovations like these.

I suspect widespread use of smart cards is only a few years away. I'm thinking not only of the magnetic strip cards we'll be using in place of paper gift certificates, which I mentioned earlier, but also of credit cards with embedded microchips. These types of cards are already in place in Europe, and it's just a matter of time before the United States follows. Smart cards could have a big impact on the way our guests pay for products, so our leadership is watching this technology closely.

Leadership is also taking a close look at electronic commerce. E-commerce is attracting a lot of attention, and rightly so, because it introduces a whole new form of retailing. It's probably too early to speculate how Meijer will implement e-commerce, but I'm looking forward to seeing how we're able to serve guests with this exciting new technology.

Maintaining our competitive advantage requires significant investments, especially when we employ new technologies, but I believe these changes are a necessity for us. Eventually, we will find a way to profit from them.

Many of our biggest steps forward came when we invested heavily in a good idea, like the Thrifty Acres concept and our automated Lansing warehouse. The lesson for leadership is clear.

Sure, big investments are a risk. However, not making them is an even greater risk. When I review Meijer's past, I see that many of our biggest steps forward came when we invested heavily in a good idea, like the Thrifty Acres concept and our automated Lansing warehouse. The lesson for leadership is clear.

Sometimes our changes will be right on target with what our guests want, other times we'll miss the mark. On occasion, we'll need the courage to stick with good ideas even when they do not succeed at first. There is no question our guests did not comprehend the Thrifty Acres concept when we introduced it. We believed in the concept, though, and stuck with it while we educated people on the utility and convenience of our revolutionary retail concept. Eventually, Thrifty Acres took hold and became the foundation for today's Meijer store.

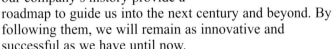

Meijer needs to remain known as the place where the future happens first, and happens in a guest-friendly way. The lessons learned throughout our company's history provide a roadmap to guide us into the next century and beyond. By following them, we will remain as innovative and successful as we have until now.

EPILOGUE

Jim McLean

To say that Earl Holton has come and gone from Meijer could not be further from the truth. He lives in the spirit of the organization he led, in the careers he nurtured, and in the lives he's influenced over the years, including mine.

What is it about Earl that has made him a strong leader, a sought-after adviser, a valued citizen?

To begin with, Earl has rare business gifts. He is able to see things that others can't — or don't — and anticipates the unanticipated. Where others might find surprises, Earl can foresee challenge or opportunity. He can quickly and astutely assess a concept or strategy and determine whether it is appropriate and sound. He is able to empower others to carry plans forward effectively. He is a man of vision and intelligence; a teacher and a standard-bearer of the highest order. More importantly, he is a man of values, of ethical conviction, whose beliefs and practices are rooted in dignity and compassion for his fellow man. This is evident in everything he does.

It is not by coincidence that many corporations and organizations vie to name Earl to their governing boards. In fact, it is not uncommon for people and organizations throughout the community to turn to both Earl and Donnalee for support and advice. They know they can count on the Holtons to offer genuine concern and thoughtful assistance for their needs and causes.

As history has clearly established, Earl and Donnalee answer the call for service — in their communities, with business associates, for their friends and family — with eagerness, wisdom, and grace. We have witnessed the meaning of compassion and selfless service in both of them.

From Earl, I also have learned the business values and ethics I revere most. I can best illustrate these by sharing two occasions when Earl made a profound impression upon me.

One came during the Meijer 1998 Professional Development Seminar, an annual gathering of our store directors. At this event, the store directors offered a tribute to Earl and Donnalee, and they praised Earl for demanding adherence to high standards — for teaching that "standards are not negotiable." This praise came from the same team members held accountable for maintaining those lofty ideals — the very people whose success is measured by that often-challenging yardstick. Yet their words were of praise, not complaint; of admiration, not frustration. With great pride and emotion, they thanked their leader for holding us all accountable to high, "non-negotiable" standards because they know that as a result, they work for a better and stronger company.

Another of my lessons from Earl occurred as we made the decision to close our SourceClub Membership Warehouse Division. It was one of the toughest business decisions we have faced in recent years. Worse, we announced it just before the holiday season. In a room crowded with SourceClub team members, in a time of great emotion, the question was inevitably posed: "Why are you giving us this news just before the Christmas season?"

Earl did not respond with an explanation of the agonizing debate that went on for months, of the business and financial determinants, the discussion that led up to the decision, or the endless hand-wringing. He said simply, "Because it is the honest thing to do."

Honesty. It is as integral to who Earl Holton is as it is to what he does. The business decision to close the division had been made, he explained. It simply would have been unfair — dishonest, even — to go forward pretending that it had not. It was a difficult decision, made even more difficult by its timing. But it was the honest thing to do.

In the aftermath of this event, a number of my SourceClub acquaintances found that, indeed, it had been the right decision at the right time. It was the best thing for the company, and it enabled team members to move ahead more quickly with their lives and take their careers in new directions. Delaying the inevitable might have hindered their ability to be successful in their career moves. Seeing things others cannot and anticipating the unanticipated — these are gifts that often are more rewarding in the long run, gifts for which people are appreciative in retrospect. We are fortunate Earl used and shouldered them so well.

Earl has been a remarkable teacher. I will always cherish the lessons I learned from him, and hope to do him service by using them well. And just in case Earl thinks he can rest now, I have secured his e-mail address, his fax and telephone numbers, and his itinerary as far out as possible to make sure I have adequately planned on getting advice from the man who is my most effective business adviser.

The Meijer family, the executive leadership team, and Meijer team members

Jim McLean and Earl, 1998

will miss Earl's day-to-day involvement in our company and the immediate availability of his wisdom and advice. But we are reassured by his conviction that he has prepared us well to move forward and write the next chapters of Meijer. We are grateful for his confidence and hope we not only live up to, but exceed his expectations of us. We hope we can continue to build Meijer in the same spirit and tradition and with the same vigor as Earl has consistently displayed.

As inadequate as it may seem, on behalf of all who have been touched by you, Earl, we say, "Thanks!"

MEMORABLE MOMENTS